50 HIKING TRAILS
PORTLAND &
NORTHWEST OREGON

By Don & Roberta Lowe

The Touchstone Press
P.O. Box 81
Beaverton, Oregon 97075

I.S.B.N. 0-911518-70-3
Copyright © 1986
by Don and Roberta Lowe

Japanese Gardens

Indian Beach, Oregon Coast

Elowah Falls, Columbia River Gorge

Mt. Hood from the summit of Larch Mountain

introduction

In what metropolitan area do people have the option of heading west to the beach, east to the mountains or even remaining in the city when they're planning a hike? Portland, Oregon, of course. In fact, they can even continue a bit farther east and visit the desert setting of Smith Rock State Park and return the same day. And Oregon hikers have many of these options throughout the year. Coastal and city hikes are always open and, except in the most severe winters, the three routes in the Coast Range, several trails in the Columbia Gorge and a few in the Cascades are snow covered for only a couple of months.

With a change of 6,000 feet in elevation there's obviously a great variety of scenery, from the forested headlands above the perpetual surging ocean, to the gentle woods of the city to the high slopes where only wind warped and stunted trees survive. Yet there's also a continuity in this variety: the sand along the shoreline and the volcanic ash on Mt. Hood; the sound of the wind through the tree limbs, ponderous at sea level and whistling at timberline; and the Indian paintbrush and lupine that bloom as colorfully on alpine slopes as they do at sea level.

The only characteristic all 50 hikes in this guide share is that they can be done as one day trips from the Portland area. Aside from that, they cover the gamut for length, difficulty and scenic features. A section of a city hike could be walked between a late lunch and an early dinner; a few trips are relatively short and easy but more driving time is needed to reach them; others offer a moderate workout; and a couple are so strenuous they demand all your endurance and even some route finding. Because their destinations connect with other routes, three of the trips (No's. 34, 47 and 48) also make excellent backpacks.

Thirty nine of these trails have never before seen the black of print in a hiker's guide. Eight (No's. 1, 2, 3, 5, 7, 8, 14 and 16) of the remaining eleven first appeared in *100 Oregon Hiking Trails*, which has been unavailable for over a decade, but they have changed so much the write-ups that appear in this book are essentially new. Only the route up Saddle Mountain (No. 7) in the Coast Range has remained the same, except for the removal of the fire lookout on its summit. The four hikes in this guide for which portions can be found in another book in print (*35 Hiking Trails — Columbia River Gorge*) are No's. 17, 18, 20 and 21. These are part of the new 30 mile long Gorge Trail that, to date, extends from Bridal Veil east to the Columbia Gorge Work Center.

If you hike once a week, every week, this guide can last you three years. This is how: by methodically planning your trips you make all 50 the first year. During winter there are, without fail, several weeks of clear weather. Everyplace else is snow covered, or at least bleak, but the beaches always look the same and the coastal headlands, with their preponderance of evergreens don't change that much with the seasons. So these weeks are the perfect time to enjoy the shore. The first wildflowers and green buds of spring are going to appear along the city trails and a walk then is a real morale booster. Next, the spring show begins in the Gorge and the hiking there continues to be superb into June. Then it's time to move into the Cascades and do higher and higher routes as the summer progresses. Around the end of September reverse the order, first returning to the Gorge, then to the city and finally the beach. For the second year you enjoy the hikes in a different time of the year. Most trails have at least two times every year when they are especially attractive. For example, Neahkahnie Mountain (No. 3) is perfect for one of those clear, calm balmy winter days but it also supports a delightful garden of wildflowers from late May through early June. All those green buds that unfurled in the spring throughout the city and in the Gorge turn yellows, peachy reds and golds in the autumn. And the alpine country that was exhuberant with bright blooms and lush meadows in early August takes on a different spectrum of more elegant hues two months later. For the third year you take the hikes in less than ''perfect'' conditions. A forest of conifers and blooming rhododendrons is exquisite in misty weather. The snow may be a nuisance to walk over but the white of the ground, the red bark and green boughs of massive cedars and a blue sky overhead will create an image you'll never forget. High alpine slopes are dramatic in dense fog. Since you already know what the views are, you can enjoy the mysteriously romantic setting without fretting that you're missing anything. There are some exceptions to this all weather hiking: don't do a brushy hike when it's wet nor a cross-country one when it's not clear. And don't risk having your car snowed in at a trailhead.

Keep in mind that once you leave freeways and main roads travel is going to be slower. Twenty of the hikes, primarily in the northern Oregon Cascades section, follow unpaved roads for the final distances to the trailheads. Although, with a couple of exceptions, these routes have good surfaces, they are going to necessitate even slower driving.

Note that the earlier in the spring you hike, particularly in the Gorge and the remainder of the Cascades, the more likely you are to precede the work crews that clear blowdown, slides and other impedimenta. On cross country trips or on trails not on any official trail system, there will never be any maintenance, except that done by people using the route. If you're interested in doing trail maintenance or construction volunteer work, contact the local land management agency for the area you're interested in (addresses and phone numbers are on page 11 of this guide). Talk with people closest to where you want to help out. For instance, if you're interested in the Hunchback Ridge area phone the Zigzag Ranger Station, not the headquarters for the Mt. Hood National Forest. Be warned that trail maintenance and construction is hard work. It usually doesn't mean flicking limbs and pebbles off treads or snipping foliage but heavy labor like moving large rocks, digging culverts or serious pruning. Also, you should be prepared to offer several blocks of time, not just a few hours for one day.

All the trails in this guide are closed to motorized vehicles and most are closed to bicycles.

hiking in northwestern oregon

Because of the variety of hikes included in this guide the equipment you'll need will vary. If you're strolling through any of the city parks except Forest Park on a warm, dry day you can wear casual clothes and carry nothing except your wallet. For any hike, pack all valuables with you. Don't leave them in the trunk or even try to hide them because beady eyes may well be watching you from a nearby hiding place and their owners will head right for the spot after you've left. Any purloinable items that you can't take with you on a hike, such as tape decks, cassettes, etc., should be left at home. Except for the shorter city hikes, it's a good practice to include a pack filled with all the essentials: wool hat, gloves, sweater, windbreaker, waterproof garment, first aid kit, map of the area, compass (if you know how to use it), flashlight and a little extra food. An accident can happen on even the smoothest trail and the victim will need to be tended and kept warm while help is obtained. On clear days from early summer through early fall include and use a sunscreen for all hikes where you'll be in the open. Although may hikers wear athletic shoes — and they certainly are satisfactory for smooth trails — light weight hiking boots are recommended for any trip that is long, steep, rough or might be muddy. A man's large umbrella makes rainy day hikes more enjoyable. Surprisingly, they're not uncomfortable to carry and one keeps your head, torso, pack and, if you wear them, glasses dry. Another recommended accouterment is a walking cane. It's a welcome third leg while fording streams and traveling on rough terrain and can give relief to grumbling knees on steep downhill grades. One can even help you go uphill faster, if you're so inclined. Buy a model with a curved handle so you can hook it over you arm when you need both hands free.

Always leave home with adequate water. If you encounter a good water source along the hike, you can refill the bottles from it. By being prudent and not drinking water that comes from lakes and from streams that flow through camping areas or where there is livestock, hikers can usually take advantage of the fresh, cold streams and springs they might encounter along trails at the coast or in the mountains, but never in the city. But there's always the risk, even from sources that should be safe, and those warnings about Giardia aren't on the Wilderness bulletin boards for nothing. So, unless you're a bit of an informed gambler, stick to tap water. During summer you can fill plastic bottles, leaving enough room for expansion, and put them in the freezer at least one day before the hike. Most of the ice should have melted by lunch time and you'll have cold water to enjoy straight or to combine with a beverage mix.

The less popular a trail, the less abuse it suffers. This is not necessarily because fewer people use it but because those who do tend to be more knowledgeable hikers. They NEVER SHORTCUT SWITCHBACKS. Doing so can be dangerous to those below but the primary reason for the prohibition is because of the unsightly erosion channels that result. Nature does quite enough destruction without any help from humans. If you're feeling assertive you might reprimand people you see shortcutting. One rearrangement of the landscape that is encouraged is the removal of small pieces of blowdown, rocks and other debris from trails. Soccer players and those with hiking canes will be especially adept at flicking objects off the tread. What you do, trail crews won't have to and they can spend their time on larger projects. Just don't bombard hikers who might be traveling below. Not only do responsible hikers not leave litter — and that includes orange rinds and egg shells — they pick up any they might encounter. What they do leave are wildflowers so those who follow can enjoy them also. If you must defecate, do so well away from the trail and at least 200 feet from streams and lakes. Pretend you're a cat by first digging a hole and then afterwards returning the top soil and gently tamping it down. Women should carry a little plastic bag in which to put personal hygiene items and then dispose of it at home.

Aural pollution, such as shouting, radios, barking dogs, etc., doesn't belong in the outdoors any more than visual pollution.

In summary, the Golden Rule in the outdoors is Be Inconspicuous.

If you have any questions, suggestions, complaints or compliments on how the trails and terrain are being managed, write to the appropriate agencies, the addresses for which can be found on page 11 of this guide. Comments intended for the authors can be sent to them in care of The Touchstone Press, PO Box 81, Beaverton, Oregon 97075. All trails in this guide were hiked by the authors but keep in mind that conditions can change, sometimes quickly, from heavy rains causing landslides, windstorms resulting in sections of blowdown, and so on.

Good Hiking.

D.L.
R.L.

LEGEND

Trail Head	★
Trail	- - - -
Campsite	△
Mileage	5.6
Trail No.	No. 600
Road No.	6340
Primary Road	▬▬
Secondary Road	====

area map

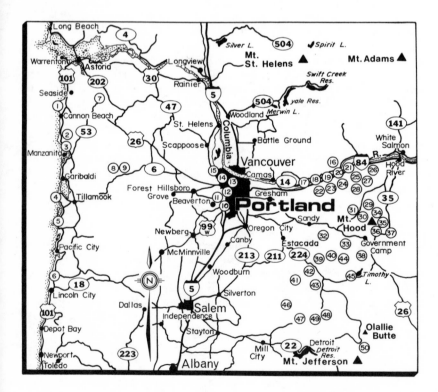

agency listings

Listed below are addresses and phone numbers for the government agencies having jurisdiction over the trails described in this guide. The relevant hike numbers are shown for each agency.

Oregon State Parks   1, 2, 3, 4, 5 and 7
3600 East Third
Tillamook, Oregon 97141
842-5501

Hebo Ranger District   6
Siuslaw National Forest
Hebo, Oregon 97122
392-3161

State of Oregon Department of Forestry   8 and 9
801 Gales Creek Road
Forest Grove, Oregon 97116
357-2191

Tryon Creek State Park   10
11321 SW Terwilliger Blvd.
Portland, Oregon 97219
636-4550

City of Portland Bureau of Parks and Recreation   11, 12, 13, 14 and 15
1120 SW 5th, Room 502
Portland, Oregon 97204
796-5193

Wind River Ranger District   16
Gifford Pinchot National Forest
Carson, Washington 98610
(509) 427-5645

Mt. Hood National Forest
2955 NW Division
Gresham, Oregon 97030
666-0700

   Columbia Gorge Ranger District   17, 18, 19, 20, 21, 22, 23, 24, 25 and 28
   31520 SE Woodard Road
   Troutdale, Oregon 97060
   695-2276

   Hood River Ranger District   26, 27, 29, 34, 35, 36 and 37
   6780 Highway 35
   Mt. Hood-Parkdale, Oregon 97041
   666-0701 (toll free from Portland)

   Zigzag Ranger District   30, 31, 32, 33 and 40
   70220 E. Highway 26
   Zigzag, Oregon 97049
   666-0704 (toll free from Portland)

   Bear Springs Ranger District   38 and 45
   Route 1 Box 65
   Maupin, Oregon 97037
   328-6211

   Estacada Ranger District   39, 41, 42, 44, 47, 48 and 49
   595 NW Industrial Way
   Estacada, Oregon 97023
   630-6861

   Clackamas Ranger District   43 & 50
   61431 E. Highway 224
   Estacada, Oregon 97023
   630-4256

Area Manager Clackamas Area   46
Bureau of Land Management
1717 Fabry Road SE
Salem, Oregon 97306
PO Box 3227
Salem, Oregon 97302
399-5646

contents

Beach below Neahkahnie Mountain

Dory near Neahkahnie

Beach at Manzanita

Nehalem Sandspit

the oregon coast

As exceptionally scenic and interesting as places like the Colorado Rockies and the desert Southwest are, they share, at least as far as Northwesterners are concerned, one major flaw: they are too many mountain ranges removed from the Pacific Ocean. Even people who don't go to the beach all that often are comforted knowing that expanse of water is nearby. And the rest of the population relishes the option of being able to head east to the mountains or west to the beach, depending on their whim and the weather.

The first six hikes in this guide are over headlands and No's. 7, 8 and 9 climb to highpoints in the Coast Range. A bonus on hike's No's. 1 through 5 is that on the same outing you can combine tromping along trails with padding along beaches. Also, these routes follow the Oregon Coast Trail, which, like the Gorge Trail (No's. 17 through 21), was created by connecting existing treads with brand new ones. Actually, long stretches of the Coast Trail required no work at all because they follow wide beaches. All the coast hikes are moderate in length and elevation gain with the exception of the uncharacteristically steep climbs of Kings (No. 8) and Elk (No. 9) Mountains.

Three superb spit hikes are not included in this guide but are highly recommended for those days when you want a level walk with lots of sand, surf, seagulls and sandpipers...and beachcombing. Four mile long Bayocean Peninsula at Tillamook Bay can be reached by trail from Cape Meares (No. 4) or you can drive directly to near the southern end. Netarts Spit extends five miles north from Cape Lookout (No. 5). The third beach walk is the 5.3 mile loop that heads south along the ocean side of the Nehalem Sandspit and returns along the bay side. Be sure to do the loop at low tide so you'll be able to hike on sand along the bay. To reach the start of the circuit, drive on US 101 to the road to Nehalem Bay State Park, located between Manzanita and Nehalem. Once in the park continue beyond the spur to the campground area and come to a junction. The route left to the boat launch is the road you'll be walking back on. Keep straight and park in front of the restroom building. A short trail heads from its northwest corner to the beach. Head south and where you come to the jetty walk northeast along its crest, assuming wave action isn't too high, toward the bay. From the end of the jetty continue along the edge of the water, occasionally climbing the low bank to see if you can spot the elk herd that winters here, to the boat launch and follow the road back to your car.

All beaches and headlands are hikeable and attractive year around. At least twice every winter are long stretches of clear, calm, often balmy weather without the mugginess of summer. Definitely plan some visits then. Cross country skiers should note that these conditions usually make for icy or, at best, crusty snow in the mountains so they can head west without lamenting they're missing any good touring. A notable exception to the generally seasonless character of the coast is the glorious profusion of spring wildflowers that bloom on Neahkahnie (No. 3) and Saddle (No. 7) Mountains.

Hikers are well aware of the ever changing character of the natural landscape and nowhere is this more obvious than along the northern Oregon coast. The peculiar concave, deciduously vegetated slopes above Ecola Point (No. 1) are the result of a massive landslide in the early 1960's. For varying lengths of time every winter the road between Ecola Point and Indian Beach is closed because it becomes so humpy from ground movement. A few years ago rockfall obliterated the south entrance of the tunnel that connects the beach at Oceanside to a superb stretch of shoreline to the north. And even when the land itself is stable, what grows on it might not be. Because of frequent strong winds and often saturated soil, coastal trees are especially subject to blowdown. In other words, even more than the Cascades, coastal trail conditions can change quickly and dramatically.

The caveats peculiar to coastal hiking are to avoid rolling logs on the beach walks when the surf is high and stay off jetties and rocks if the ocean isn't reasonably calm. Also, sections of trails on the headlands can be muddy so wear appropriate shoes.

Books about the coast are plentiful and an especially recommended one is the interesting, and often hilarious, *Tillamook Light* by James Gibbs.

1 TILLAMOOK HEAD

One day trip
Distance: 7.5 miles one way
Elevation gain: 1,600 feet; loss 1,500 feet
High point: 1,200 feet
Allow 4 hours one way
Usually open all year
Topographic map:
U.S.G.S. Cannon Beach, Oreg.
15′   1955

Tillamook Head is the immense, forested hump between Seaside and Cannon Beach. In addition to a variety of always good looking woods and periodic views of the ocean, beaches and Tillamook Rock Lighthouse, a less common feature is a short side trip to the ruins of a small WWII artillery battery. As with almost all coast hikes, it is perfect for a car shuttle and the length can be shortened, in this case by ending (or beginning) at Indian Beach instead of Ecola Point. However, the 1.5 mile stretch between these two points travels above some especially impressive seascapes which makes the extra distance worthwhile. Note that the road between Ecola Point and Indian Beach may be closed periodically in winter. Also be informed that the park closes at dusk. On weekends and holidays from Memorial Day through Labor Day a modest entrance fee is charged. Carry water.

To begin from the northern trailhead drive 2.7 miles north along US 26-101 from where they merge to the most southerly signal in Seaside. Turn west, parallel the golf course for 0.2 mile, at its west side turn left onto S. Edgewood and follow it 1.2 miles to its end at a parking area. If you're establishing a shuttle or doing the hike from south to north, drive to the north end of Cannon Beach and follow the signs to Ecola State Park. At a T-junction turn left to start (or end) the hike at Ecola Point or turn right if you're heading for Indian Beach.

At the parking area near Seaside begin the hike from the sign at the southeast corner of the turn-around. Soon curve right, come to a dirt road and walk up it for about 75 feet to the resumption of the trail on your right. Climb moderately in 16 switchbacks. At a more open area have a sighting north to Cape Disappointment in Washington, a bit farther the expanse of beach near Seaside and then a view of the town itself. Around 1.5 miles, just before the main climb is over, stay right (straight) where an unsigned path heads left. From here until the 5.0 mile point the trail is a roller coaster of small climbs and descents.

At 3.7 miles come to a large sign identifying the short spur to Clarks Viewpoint where a plaque offers interesting historical information. After winding down in nine switchbacks come to a sign pointing to restrooms. Stay left on the main trail and in about 100 feet come to an old road. To visit the battery turn right and follow the road through the clearing and then downhill for 0.1 mile.

A short distance south of the road crossing the main trail enters a blowdown salvage area whose ambience is improved during mid-summer by an exceptionally robust population of foxglove. Near 5.0 miles round the nose of a ridge and switchback down into a lush, grassy clearing dotted with big, fat alders that are a complement to the dense grove of small, slim ones at the north end of the hike.Farther on turn right at a road and follow it a couple hundred feet to the parking area at Indian Beach.

To reach Ecola Point, follow the marker at the southeast corner of the parking area, cross a bridge and turn left at the junction of the trail to the beach. Switchback a few times and contour above the beach. You'll have frequent reminders that this is a typically unstable coastal slope. Have a varied scene of woods and overlooks and near 7.2 miles come to those promised super views. Re-enter woods, climb and descend briefly and then walk mostly on the level to the parking area. If you want to explore the final short section of trail through Ecola Park, which passes two viewpoints, walk up the road, turn right — as if you were leaving the park — and look to your right (west) for the trail, which initially parallels the road.

Tillamook Rock Lighthouse

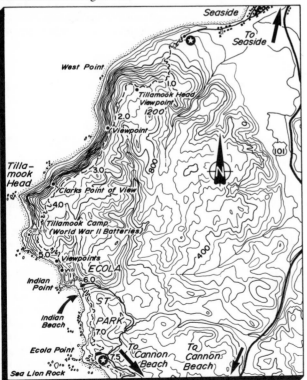

2 ARCH CAPE to SHORT SAND BEACH

One day trip
Distance: 7.2 miles one way
Elevation gain: 1,400 feet; loss 1,300 feet
(north to south)
High point: 970 feet
Allow 4 hours one way
Usually open all year
Topographic map:
U.S.G.S. Cannon Beach, Oreg.
15'   1955

After crossing Tillamook Head and traversing through Ecola State Park (No. 1), the Oregon Coast Trail follows the expanse of sand south from Cannon Beach for seven miles to the resumption of a tread on the north side of Arch Cape. This trail winds up and over the cape, crosses US 101 and then takes a circuitous route through varied woods past picture perfect Cape Falcon, Smuggler Cove and Short Sand Beach. As with most coast hikes, this outing is perfect for a car shuttle. Hikers wanting a shorter trip can end (or begin) where the trail crosses the highway. Carry water.

To reach the northernmost starting point, proceed south on US 101 from its junction with US 26 for 10.8 miles to Arch Cape — Mill Road that angles off from the east side of the highway 0.2 mile north of

the Arch Cape tunnel. Turn onto the road, after a short distance curve left and head east 0.4 mile to a short spur on the right and a sign stating *Trail*. If you're establishing a shuttle or beginning from the southernmost access point, take US 101 for 3.6 miles south of the Arch Cape tunnel or 4.1 miles north of Manzanita to the middle parking lot — the one on the east side of the highway — for Oswald West State Park. The point where the trail crosses US 101 is 1.1 miles south of the tunnel and 2.5 miles north of the parking lot.

From the end of the spur off Arch Cape — Mill Road cross a suspension bridge, come to a T-junction and turn left. Climb over the crest of the Cape and near 1.3 miles come to a logging road. Turn right, keep right farther on and continue downhill to the highway. At the gate be sure and read about the "Friday the 13th" storm of 1981.

Cross the highway and head 125 feet south to the resumption of the trail. After a descent to a creek and the climb back out come to a road, cross it and begin meandering downhill, initially paralleling US 101. Veer west along a faint old roadbed and eventually leave it at a mileage sign. Travel up among spindly trees and make a sharp left turn at an obscure sign. A few immense conifers and a good collection of fungus thrive along this next stretch.

Wind up in six irregular switchbacks to a logged crest. You'll have views north beyond Haystack Rock and Cannon Beach to Tillamook Head. Walk on the crest and then along a cat road before coming to the resumption of the trail, which eventually re-enters unmolested woods. Have a view of the ocean and follow a winding course of minor ups and downs to a viewpoint where you can see as far north as Cape Disappointment on the Washington side of the Columbia River. After more meanderings come to a viewpoint near 4.1 miles at the northwestern edge of a canyon. Look for sea lions sprawled on the rocks below.

Traverse in and out of this side canyon and cross over the neck of Cape Falcon where an unsigned, but well-used, spur heads west to its tip. As you traverse above Smuggler Cove you can see Short Sand Beach below or look ahead to a section of trail on Neahkahnie Mountain (No. 3) and beyond to the four mile long Nehalem Sandspit. Travel away from the ocean and walk through a clearcut where a sign near the far side explains the reason for it. Re-enter the woods and eventually come to an unsigned junction. The route to the left heads directly to the most northerly of the three parking lots. To reach the middle one, keep straight and descend to a picnic area just above the beach. Turn left, pass the restrooms, keeping the building to your left, cross a bridge and follow the paved trail, keeping straight (left) where two routes head right (see No. 3).

Short Sand Creek

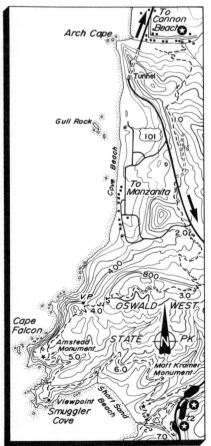

3 NEAHKAHNIE MOUNTAIN

One day trip
Distance: 3.6 miles one way to summit; 8
    miles as a loop
Elevation gain: 1,950 feet; loss 350 feet to
    summit
High point: 1,631 feet
Allow 2 hours one way to summit; 3½ hours
    as a loop
Usually open all year
Topographic maps:
  U.S.G.S. Cannon Beach, Oreg.
  15' 1955
  U.S.G.S. Nehalem, Oreg.
  15' 1955

Late May through early June is an especially fetching time for this particular trip because of the magnificent wildflower displays on the west and south slopes. Wild iris are abundant and share the space with, among other blooms, larkspur, foxglove, wild cucumber, thistle and cow parsnip.

Typical of beach trips, the Neahkahnie Mountain hike has several beginning and ending points. A car shuttle is ideal but a loop in the configuration of a figure eight is possible by returning along US 101, which is paralleled by a pedestrian path for one mile. Among other options, hikers can begin from US 101 at the 1.7 mile point or from the southernmost end of the trail and climb that side of the peak to the excellent viewpoint on the spiney summit. Begin with adequate water.

Drive on US 101 for 14.5 miles south from its junction with US 26 or 4.1 miles north of Manzanita to the most southerly of the three parking areas for Oswald West State Park. If you're establishing a shuttle, first drive both cars to an unpaved road signed with a hiker symbol and an Oregon Coast Trail post heading east 2.5 miles south of the parking area and just north of a former golf course, which is 1.6 miles north of Manzanita. Follow this side road 0.4 mile.

From the north end of the parking area at Oswald West State Park take the paved trail downhill. Keep left where a connector goes through a camp area, farther on keep left again where the fork to the right heads to the picnic area above Short Sand Beach (see No. 2) and after several yards come to Necarney Creek. Because of lack of funds, there are no plans to replace the former bridge here. If you want a somewhat easier crossing, retrace your steps and take the route to the picnic area. Walk along the beach across Necarney Creek and head through the woods to the resumption of the trail.

About 100 feet beyond the ford come to a signed fork where a spur goes right to the beach. Keep left, leaving the paved surface, and begin switchbacking uphill. Descend from the crest and at 1.4 miles come to a clearing. Keep straight, crossing an old roadbed, to the resumption of the trail and soon come to the open slopes of the headland. The next few tenths mile is the only rough and brushy tread along the hike.

Climb briefly to the highway, cross it, angling to the right, to the resumption of the trail and begin winding up the open slope. Of course, don't pick any of the wildflowers here so people who follow can also enjoy them. As you gain elevation you can see south to Cape Meares (No. 4) and Cape Lookout (No. 5) and then after a switchback north to Smuggler Cove at Short Sand Beach (No. 2). Wind up among trees to a clearing and a view of Cape Falcon, switchback and re-enter woods. Pass through an area of cleared blowdown, make three switchbacks and at 2.3 miles begin a long traverse above Necarney Creek. Switchback, eventually begin traversing along the west facing slope and have a view down onto Manzanita and Nehalem Bay. Cross a saddle and farther on switchback a few times to the open slopes of the summit ridge.

If you're doing the hike as a loop or a shuttle, follow the main trail over the narrow crest and after one switchback traverse down through woods. Have a view north to Tillamook Head (No. 1) and Rock just before re-crossing the crest and a road. Switchback seven times in woods and then make seven more turns down a treeless bush covered slope to the road.

Fog on Neahkahnie Mountain

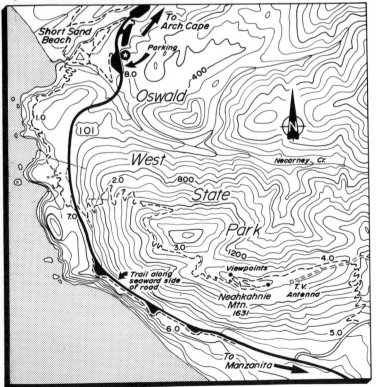

4 CAPE MEARES

One day trip
Distance: 6 miles round trip to hike all trails
Elevation gain: 1,050 feet to hike all trails
High point: 580 feet
Allow 2½ hours to hike all trails
Usually open all year
Topographic map:
U.S.G.S. Tillamook, Oreg.
15'   1955

Most of the beach hikes described in this guide offer a plethora of hiking options. The only difference with the several possible itineraries over Cape Meares is that they are all considerably shorter than their neighbors. However, the scenic attractions are not proportionally diminished and include a lighthouse with exhibits open to the public, views north, south and out to sea, the candelabra shaped Octopus Tree, an immense spruce and an aerial-like view over Bayocean Sandspit. People who want a longer hike could walk north along this 4.0 mile long peninsula, one of the most attractive on the coast. Before or after the hike, you're encouraged to visit the Pioneer Museum in Tillamook. Hikers will be especially impressed with its natural history collections.

From the center of Tillamook drive west on Third Street, following the signs to Cape Meares and Three Capes Scenic Loop, for 1.7 miles to a junction just beyond a bridge. Turn right and travel along the south edge of Tillamook Bay, which is generously populated with may varieties of waterfowl. Be sure to stop at the signs at the 5.0 mile post to read about the former resort community of Bayocean. For more about the town you can read Bert Webber's, *What Happened at Bayocean: Is Salishan Next?* Three-tenths mile farther turn left, still following the sign to Cape Meares, climb for 2.0 miles to the junction of the spur to the Cape and turn right. If you wish, you can begin the hike here. Otherwise, continue along the spur for 0.6 mile to its end.

To visit the lighthouse, follow either of the paved paths that head west from the turnaround. During early morning and at dusk you'll most likely see a good number of small brown rabbits grazing in the grass.

To take the route along the north side of the cape and down to the beach, begin at the Oregon Coast Trail post at the north edge of the turnaround. (Fill your bottles first, if necessary, because there are no water sources along the trails.) Immediately enter the woods and follow a circuitous route with minor climbs and descents to a bridge. Farther on begin traversing around a knoll and have the first of the views to the north. Several yards beyond a switch-back pass the signed 100 yard spur to the Big Spruce. Less than 0.1 mile beyond that junction the main route passes the little connector to the entrance to the park.

The main trail continues downhill and soon comes to unobstructed views north. Wind down along the edge of a clearcut. Man is not entirely responsible for the ravaged appearance of the slopes — many trees on this portion of the cape were felled by strong winds, not chainsaws. Re-enter woods, again pass the edge of the clearcut, make a few short switch-backs and come to a signed junction. Turn left and walk the 50 feet to near the water's edge. If you want to continue farther north along the spit but the tide is too high, retrace your route the 50 feet to the junction and continue north along the Oregon Coast Trail, which eventually meets the more sandy portion of the peninsula.

To explore the southern 0.6 mile of trail on Cape Meares head to the restroom building above the east side of the parking area and just beyond it veer right and follow an ill defined tread south to the Octopus Tree, whose exotic configuration is explained by a sign. From the tree follow along the edge of the wire fence to the beginning of an obvious trail. Traverse along the open, south facing slope into a side canyon, cross a bridge and continue gradually uphill to the road. The Oregon Coast Trail doesn't become a trail proper again until the north side of Cape Lookout.

The Octopus Tree at Cape Meares

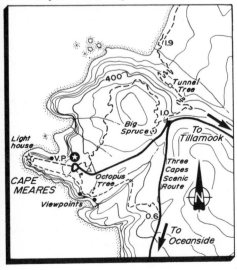

5 CAPE LOOKOUT

One day trip
Distance: 2.5 miles to Cape Lookout from
crest; 2.3 miles to northern beach
from crest; 1.5 miles to southern
beach from crest
Elevation gain: 200 feet; loss 770 feet to
Cape Lookout from crest;
800 feet loss from crest to
northern and southern
beaches
High point: 800 feet
Allow 1½ hours to Cape Lookout from crest
one way; 1 hour from crest to
northern beach; ½ hour from crest
to southern beach
Usually open all year
Topographic map:
U.S.G.S. Tillamook, Oreg.
15′   1955

Cape Lookout shares many characteristics with the four previous hikes over headlands in this guide (No's. 1, 2, 3 and 4): Several beginning points, a chance to pad along a beach or two and perfect for a car shuttle. However, unlike the relative snub-nosed headlands those other trails cross, Cape Lookout has a long snout. From the parking lot at the crest a trail goes to the tip where the view extends south past Cape Kiwanda to Cascade Head (see No. 6). Also from that parking area, one trail winds down to park facilities and the five mile long beach on the north side of the cape while another switchbacks south to a more secluded stretch of sand. Carry water, particularly for the routes that head west and south.

From the center of Tillamook follow the sign pointing to Three Capes Scenic Loop. At the junc-

tion you come to after 1.7 miles you can keep left and head south 8.5 miles to the entrance to Cape Lookout State Park but for a more scenic, though longer route, keep right and follow along the edge of Tillamook Bay where you're guaranteed sightings of copious numbers and varieties of birds. Following the signs identifying the Three Capes Scenic Loop will take you past Cape Meares (No. 4) and Oceanside to the entrance to Cape Lookout State Park.

If you're beginning from the lower, northerly trail, keep right and drive 0.6 mile to the end of the road at the picnic area. To reach the parking area on the crest, stay left at the park entrance and continue another 2.7 miles to a sign pointing west to Cape Lookout Trail parking. If you're approaching from the south, this crest is about 5.0 miles from Sand Lake.

Hikers starting from (or ending at) the northerly, beach level trail should be sure to stop just southwest of the parking lot and read the plaques about the geology and plant and animal life in the area. From the markers walk south along a very wide path for several hundred yards to the beginning of the trail proper. After a short distance come to a T-junction, turn right and 100 yards farther keep left where a spur heads down to the sand. After four switchbacks travel above the beach. In addition to the views down onto the surf and north up the coastline, during winter you'll enjoy the sight of good sized waterfalls shooting from the cliffs into the ocean. Re-enter woods and about midway along the climb come to a connector on your left that meets the highway in 200 yards. Descend into a side canyon and be careful as you cross the bridge here because it's slick. Wind up an erratic grade for the remaining mile to the crest.

To hike out along Cape Lookout head west from the upper parking area. After a few yards pass the trail that heads down to the north and 75 yards farther come to the junction of the shorter route to the south side of the headland. The trail out to the tip of the promontory crosses several times from the north to south sides so you'll have views in both directions and uphill and level stretches give your legs a rest from the mostly downhill. During summer, lupine and Indian paintbrush, those adaptable plants that thrive in various guises from sea level to timberline, brighten the open slopes just before the end. Do *not* follow the use path down from the tip as it is extremely steep and slippery.

If not now, you're urged on a future hike to take the trail that heads down to the south from the crest. It winds through a variety of woods in about two dozen irregularly spaced switchbacks to the beach. During low tide you can follow the beach south for 4.0 miles to Sand Lake.

Looking down western tip of Cape Lookout

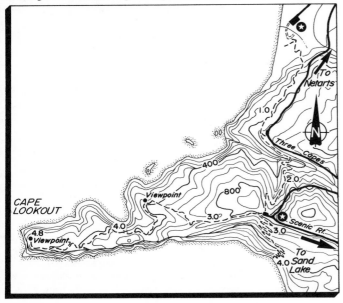

6 HARTS COVE

One day trip
Distance: 2.6 miles one way
Elevation gain: 200 feet; loss 1,000 feet
High point: 1,050 feet
Allow 1½ hours one way .
Usually open all year
Topographic map:
  U.S.G.S. Hebo, Oreg.
  7.5′   1955

The Harts Cove Trail has a split personality. Except for one short stretch where the accoustics are just right for sounds of surf and barking seals and sea lions and for one viewpoint at 1.4 miles, the route could be a most pleasant woodsy outing far from the ocean. Then, with no transition, the final few tenths mile are along a glorious, grassy headland. You'll definitely want to spend an uncommonly

long time at its tip watching the waves crashing against the walls of Harts Cove.

The Harts Cove Trail is the most northerly of the three routes in the Cascade Head area and, unlike the other two, which are on Nature Conservancy property, it's on US Forest Service land, the only one in this guide's coast section that is. After prolonged rains, sections of the Harts Cove Trail can be even muddier than the other beach routes, so wear boots — not tennis or low-cut shoes.

Drive on US 101 for 3.4 miles south of Neskowin or about 3.5 miles north of the junction of Oregon 18 and US 101 to unpaved road 1861 heading west just south of the crest. Turn onto it, after 2.6 miles keep left, staying on 1861. Continue along it for another 1.9 miles, passing the beginning of the more northerly of the two Nature Conservancy routes, to the end of 1861 and the signed beginning of the Harts Cove Trail.

Immediately begin descending and soon make the first of five switchbacks. Curve into a side canyon and cross Cliff Creek. Beyond the stream begin climbing at a varied, but always moderate grade. Because of their location, some slopes and ridges are repeatedly and severely affected by strong winds. Much of the Harts Cove Trail traverses such vulnerable terrain. A tangle of blowdown covered sections of the route during the late 1970's. The tread was completely tidied up and then the next year the awesome "Friday the 13th" storm of 1981 (see No. 2) struck, putting the trail back to square one. All that blowdown was cleared away but, sooner or later, there will be yet another storm and...

Around 1.1 miles you may hear those seals and sea lions. Stop to read the informative sign about the forest and just beyond it come to the viewpoint where you can look across the narrow inlet of Harts Cove to the grassy headland that is your destination. Although it is close, as the crow flies, you still have a bit over a mile of hiking to go.

Travel north along the face of the slope and then curve east into a large side canyon holding Chitwood Creek. Eventually, cross the stream, climb at an increasingly gradual grade for 0.6 mile before abruptly coming to the edge of the woods and the beginning of the open headland. Extensive work on the Harts Cove Trail was begun in 1984 and a few sections of the tread were rebuilt. Probably the only relocation obvious to hikers familiar with the route is that the point where the trail now meets the grass is a bit farther south than the previous alignment.

Note where you leave the woods so you can find the trail on the way back and follow the path down the headland to a small level area near its tip. Although the view extends north to Cape Lookout (No. 5) and west far out to sea, the most captivating scenes are the headland itself and into Harts Cove.

Harts Cove

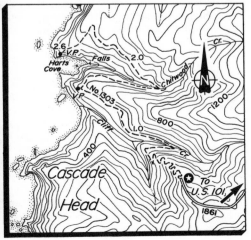

7 SADDLE MOUNTAIN

One day trip
Distance: 3.4 miles one way
Elevation gain: 1,900 feet
High point: 3,283 feet
Allow 1½ hours one way
Usually open March through December
Topographic map:
  U.S.G.S. Saddle Mountain, Oreg.
  15′   1955

Saddle Mountain at the northern end of the Coast Range is one of those hikes for which either the route itself or the destination would merit a visit. The trail winds past massive outcroppings eroded into fantastic formations not quite like any other in Oregon. From the former lookout site on the summit eyes seem to first notice the mouth of the Columbia River and then they take in the other landmarks, which include lots of ocean to the west, the Olympic Mountains to the north and the major peaks from a surprisingly close Mt. Ranier south to Mt. Jefferson. Although the climb of Saddle Mountain offers varied delights throughout most of the year,

be sure to make one visit around the second to third week in June when the route passes an impressive variety of wildflowers. The only time the trip shouldn't be made is when snow or ice covers any portion of the peak because there are several exposed sections of trail. Be assured these places normally present no problems in non-winter conditions. Include extra clothing because the summit often is windy. Carry adequate water.

Drive on US 26 for 44 miles west of its junction with Oregon 6 to a sign pointing to Saddle Mountain State Park a couple hundred feet east of the 10 mile post. Turn north and drive 7.3 miles along a paved road to its end at a picnic area.

The trail, which is paved for only the first 150 yards, begins from the east side of the parking turnaround and climbs through an especially attractive grove of red alder. At 0.3 mile come to a wide, unsigned trail on your right. This 0.2 mile spur passes a view of Astoria and, just before ending at the top of a rock outcropping, affords a look at the impressive south face of Saddle Mountain. You'll be able to make out the bridge at the notch below the main peak and the black, stick like silhouettes of any hikers negotiating the final pitch.

Near where you begin switchbacking Douglas fir begin to outnumber the alder. Above one of the turns near 1.5 miles a long, thin volcanic outcropping, rather like a stone fence, extends upslope. Geologists think that the material making up this and other dikes was formed after the main rock of the peak, which is composed mostly of volcanic breccia. At the time it was formed, the shoreline was probably not far off to the east. Subsequent uplift of the area and stream erosion of less resistant material resulted in the present prominence of Saddle Mountain and neighboring highpoints.

Switchback near the dike and soon begin hiking across open slopes. Flowers you'll enjoy include monkeyflower, iris, larkspur, Indian paintbrush, phlox, buttercup, wallflower, cow parsnip, white and lavendar colored aster and columbine. Of course, don't pick any of them. When you have your first view of the ocean you'll most likely be surprised how close it is. Also, at one point you can peer 1,200 feet directly down onto the parking area. Farther on descend briefly to the bridge at the little notch and then begin the 0.5 mile climb to the top. Although from a distance the route up the bald summit block seems ill-defined, in fact, following it demands no route finding.

The lookout that stood near the north end of the summit was removed about a decade ago. You'll be able to identify Willapa Bay and Cape Disappointment north of the Columbia River, the Astor Column in Astoria and, along the coast, Tillamook Head (No. 1) and Nehalem Bay.

Saddle Mountain

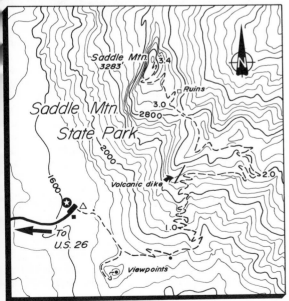

8 KINGS MOUNTAIN

One day trip
Distance: 2.7 miles one way
Elevation gain: 2,550 feet
High point: 3,226 feet
Allow 1½ to 2 hours one way
Usually open March through December
Topographic map:
   U.S.G.S. Enright, Oreg.
   15'   1955

Making the occasionally very steep climb to the summit of Kings Mountain on the way to or from the beach is an excellent complement to ambles along the ocean's edge. While resting on the grassy summit ridge you'll be rewarded with views of Mounts Hood, St. Helens and Adams, a few patches of ocean and, in the Coast Range, Saddle Mountain (No. 7) to the north and Mt. Hebo to the south. Because of the grade along the final section don't attempt the hike in snowy or icy conditions. It would also be prudent to stay off the peak during deer and elk hunting seasons. Begin with adequate water.

From the junction of US 26 and Oregon 6 about 22 miles west of Portland follow Oregon 6, the Wilson River Highway, approximately 27 miles to a sign with a hiker symbol on the south side of the highway and trail sign across the road marking the beginning of the route. These signs are 0.2 mile east of the 25 mile post.

Walk up an old road through an alder grove for 0.4 mile and then begin traveling along a trail, which from time to time again follows former road grades. Have a very brief respite, farther on have another level stretch, a wee bit of downhill and then climb gradually through more open terrain to another old roadbed. Turn right, later veer left, per a sign, and eventually begin traversing northeast.

Switchback twice, continue heading east and then curve west and come to a ridge crest. Follow along it and then begin the final 0.7 mile of often very steep uphill to the summit ridge. Trails and roads connect to Elk Mountain (No. 9) to the east.

As you gain elevation on this hike and see more gray snags you are increasingly reminded that this area was in the heart of the Tillamook Burn. On August 14, 1933, sparks generated by a felled tree being dragged over an old log ignited tinder dry ground cover. The next day winds carried flaming debris from this Gales Creek logging operation 15 miles south to the Wilson River. For the next nine days the severity of the ever spreading spot fires waxed and waned, depending on weather conditions. Then on the 24th, following a resurgence of the east winds and the lowest humidity since it began, the fire blew up. Clouds billowed up to 40,000 feet, ships 500 miles out to sea were pelted with burning debris and pastures around Tillamook were covered with three inches of ash. Amazingly, only one person was killed, crushed by a tree uprooted by the hurricane force winds of the blow up.

By the 27th the fire was confined to the ground and on the 28th of August began a week of calm, gently wet weather. An area about one-half the size of Rhode Island had been destroyed — timber, wildlife, fish, homes, barns. Flames had come within 3.5 miles of Wheeler and a mile of Forest Grove. In August 1939 another large fire began almost at the same place in Gales Creek canyon and spread to within 4.5 miles of Tillamook; in July, 1945 yet another fire started at Gales Creek and burned eight weeks before being doused by rain. In July, 1951 a final large fire began in the old burn but it was out in five days. As a result of the demand for timber created by WWII most of the salvageable timber ultimately was logged. Because of extensive hand replanting, the slopes of the Coast Range now support a new forest of Douglas fir. It's only on the steeper, less hospitable mountainsides that reminders of the conflagration remain. To read more about the Tillamook Burn refer to J. Larry Kemp's *Epitaph for the Giants.*

Kings Mountain from Oregon Highway 6

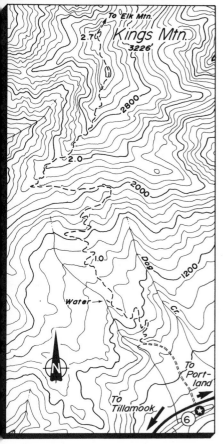

9 ELK MOUNTAIN

One day trip
Distance: 2 miles one way
Elevation gain: 2,100 feet; loss 150 feet
High point: 2,900 feet
Allow 1½ to 2 hours one way
Usually open late February through
      December
Topographic map:
  U.S.G.S. Timber, Oreg.
   15′   1955

As any hiker quickly learns, the elevation gain is as important as the distance in determining the difficulty of an outing. The climb to Elk Mountain in the Coast Range just east of Kings Mountain (No. 8) is a good example of not rating a hike entirely by its length. Although only 2.0 miles long, the route rises 2,100 vertical feet and most of them are gained in the first mile. Although most efficiently combined with a trip to the beach, the trailhead isn't so far from Portland that you couldn't justify the drive solely for the hike.

For such a short trip there are a number of caveats. It can be a hot climb during the warmest part of the summer. However, because of the exposure along much of the route, absolutely don't attempt it after prolonged rains or if snow or ice covers the slopes. Be sure to wear shoes with some kind of traction sole and begin with adequate water as you'll pass no streams. Finally, most hikers will want to stay off any trail in the Coast Range, except for Saddle Mountain (No. 7), during deer and elk hunting seasons.

Drive about 22 miles west of Portland on US 26 to the junction of Oregon 6 to Tillamook and follow Oregon 6 for 24.3 miles to signs identifying Elk Creek Forest Park, Elk Creek Road and Hikers Trail. This is at milepost 28, which indicates the mileage east of Tillamook. Turn north and follow the dirt road 0.3 mile to the picnic area and park here.

Continue along the road on foot for about 150 feet, crossing the bridge over Elk Creek, to a sign on your left marking the beginning of the Elk Mountain Trail. Climb for a few yards, turn left and traverse up through an alder grove to the nose of a ridge and a sign indicating the trail turns right. Now the serious climbing begins. Although the grade will be extreme for much of the next mile, the tread improves after about 0.1 mile. Unless you inadvertently miss the junctions, veer off to the right at two forks, traverse, switchback left and rejoin the steeper use paths that continued up the nose of the ridge. Those traverses are easier and, more importantly, following them keeps the official route from being overgrown. Because you gain elevation so quickly and the terrain is mostly open, you'll soon have views down to Elk Creek canyon around your starting point and sections of Oregon 6 and the Wilson River.

Pass another good viewpoint at a little patch of level ground and soon after it have a short downhill. Near 0.9 mile come to a levelish stretch covered by a grove of small Douglas fir. You'll most likely see evidence of elk here and beyond the trees you'll be able to see the summit of Kings Mountain. Lose more elevation as the trail traverses down the open south face of the ridge. The summit of Elk Mountain is first visible along this drop.

Resume climbing, walk on the level through another more densely forested stretch and then make the final short uphill pitch to the flat, grassy summit. Mt. Adams is the snowy hulk to the east. If you're making the hike from spring through summer you should check your clothing and body for ticks now and again when you return to your car.

If you're interested in continuing along trails and roads to Kings Mountain or exploring any of the other trails that begin from the Wilson River Highway between Gales Creek and the Kings Mountain trailhead, write to the State of Oregon Department of Forestry, 801 Gales Creek Road, Forest Grove, Oregon 97116 and ask for the pamphlet *Tillamook Forest Trails*.

Elk Mountain

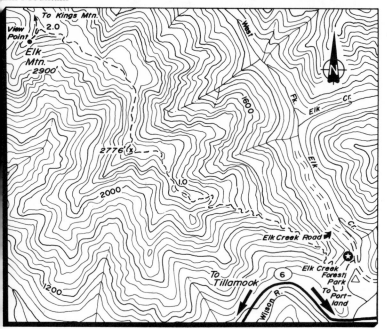

Nature House, Tryon Creek State Park

Old ruins in Balch Canyon

Wildwood Trail below the Pittock Mansion

city of portland

Because of the streets that wind and intertwine over the West Hills, particularly, Portland would provide excellent hikes even if there wasn't a single trail. The varieties of trees, bushes and flowers enjoyed from the sidewalks and road shoulders are greater than in any natural woods and surely there are more squirrels in those domestic trees. Behind all the vegetation are homes that are among the most impressive in the city and the variety of their architectural styles is almost as great as that of the plants. Distant scenes can be glimpsed beyond limbs and eaves and frequently the streets pass unobstructed viewpoints where panoramas extend east over Portland to the peaks of the Cascades. Stairways connect many streets and not only are they a delight to explore they also increase the variety of loops walkers may make. In addition to the street walks is the popular Terwilliger Bike Path (which is fine for all non-motorized travel except bicycles) that follows the serpentine alignment of SW Terwilliger Blvd. past many viewpoints from Duniway Park south to near SW Barbur Blvd. Walks with an entirely different character follow along the west bank of the Willamette River for sections between the Broadway and Sellwood Bridges.

Ah, but in addition to those wonderful walks on pavement, there are miles of real hiking trails through real woods. The expanse of tree covered slopes extending northwest above the Willamette River from Northwest Portland comprises Forest Park (No's. 14 and 15), by far the largest of the parks in this city — or almost any urban area, for that matter. Traversing about three-quarters of the way up these slopes for over one half the length of Forest Park is the Wildwood Trail. And branching from this main route are about a dozen side ones, most of which can be combined to make loops back to the Wildwood Trail. Actually, the Wildwood Trail begins three contiguous parks to the south at the World Forestry Center in the Zoo-OMSI complex. The route winds through a corner of Washington Park, among the plantings of Hoyt Arboretum (No. 12) and then past the Pittock Mansion and down through Macleay Park (No. 13) before entering Forest Park proper. Although not contiguous, the Marquam Hill-Sam Jackson Trails (No. 11) between Duniway Park and Council Crest are accessible from the World Forestry Center by streets and a new trail (see the final paragraph of this introduction for details). Farther south near Lewis & Clark College is Tryon Creek State Park (No. 10). Its 8.0 miles of trails — 12 counting the bike path — seem triple that distance because the trail system is so interconnecting, thus making possible all sorts of loop trips and variations.

From a strictly practical perspective, city hikes are perfect for when you want fresh air, exercise and pleasing scenery but don't want to take — or don't have — the time to drive far. In fact, you don't have to drive at all because buses go the the Zoo-OMSI complex, past Duniway Park, near Tryon Creek State Park and along NW Thurman St., which passes the headquarters for Forest Park and ends near the beginning of Leif Erikson Drive.

The city hikes are open all year and, unlike those along the coast, exhibit well defined seasons. You don't want to be out in any woods in an ice or wind storm but do visit one of the city trails when there's a light cover of snow. The scene is enchanting, expecially later in the day when any nearby street and house lights are on. Speaking of signs of civilization, these city hikes along trails are surprisingly outdoorsy. Certainly, you'll see some homes (and posh ones at that), cross roads on all but one of the hikes and as you head farther north into Forest Park hear the couplings of trains but, if you even think about it at all, you'll be pleasantly surprised to find how insulated you are from the sights and sounds of the city.

Eventually, a system known as the 40 Mile Loop will circle Portland, connecting existing trails, bike paths, greenways, etc. Since it will have Gresham as its eastern boundary and the Columbia River as the northern, obviously the 40 Mile Loop, when completed, is going to be considerably longer than its name indicates.

To follow the newest section of the 40 Mile Loop, which was completed in the fall of 1985, you can begin from its upper end on SW Patton Road a few yards north of its junction with SW Dosch Road and SW Humphrey Blvd. or from the lower end at the World Forestry Center. For the latter, follow SW Knights Road north from the big sign marking the start of the Wildwood Trail for several yards to a path heading left. Follow it 100 feet to a 40 Mile Loop sign and turn left. Wind down to a road, cross a bridge over SW Canyon Road, turn left and after several hundred feet come to the resumption of a trail on your right that mostly climbs for 0.5 mile to SW Patton Road.

10 TRYON CREEK STATE PARK

One day trip
Distance: See Map
Elevation gain: 1,000 feet maximum
　　　　　　　depending on route
High point: 400 feet
Allow ½ hour to all day, depending on route
Usually open all year
Topographic map:
　U.S.G.S. Lake Oswego, Oreg.
　7.5'　1961

Houses would surely be covering the 640 plus wooded acres of Tryon Creek State Park near Lewis and Clark College if it weren't for the Friends of Tryon Creek Park who in 1969 raised money for purchasing the land and convinced the State to include it in its park system. Most of the network of trails was constructed in a weekend blitz by volunteers working under the supervision of a few professionals. So, today the slopes support, in addition to the 8.0 miles of trails (4.0 more counting the bike path), a forest of coniferous and deciduous trees, an astounding variety of birds and an assortment of small mammals — even a few furtive beavers allegedly inhabit the area.

As with all Portland city hikes (No's. 10 through 15), early April when the trilliums, wood violets, skunk cabbages and other first wildflowers of the year unfurl is a particularly special time. But on a warm summer day a stroll beneath the canopy of soothing green leaves is pleasant, too. And all that deciduous foliage makes for great fall color in late October. Then, of course, in winter when all the high country trails are snow covered, the urban ones are faithfully there to be trod upon.

As is typical of city hikes, all manner of loop trips are possible in Tryon Creek State Park. The main trails have good surfaces but some of the most westerly connectors to streets can be muddy in wet weather.

Before or after the hike you're encouraged to visit Nature House just west of the main parking area. It contains exhibits, books and other information about the plants and animals in the park. Nature House is open all week and during the summer nature talks and walks begin there at 1:00 and 3:00 on Saturdays and Sundays. As you enjoy Nature House and the park keep in mind that the Friends of Tryon Creek Park are still very much involved in nurturing the object they created.

Be aware of the following rules for park use: It closes at dusk; dogs must be kept on a leash; no fires are permitted and picnicking is allowed only in the shelter north of Nature House; no plant or animal collecting is permitted; stay on the official trials — use paths anywhere disrupt the natural trails and, if they become worn enough, hikers may inadvertently take them and reinforce the errant treads.

Although trails end at many different roads that can be good access points for people living in the area and those already familiar with the park, generally the best place to begin is from the main parking area midway along the eastern boundary. Take SW Terwilliger Blvd. 1.1 miles south of its junction with SW Boones Ferry Road or 1.5 miles north of its junction with Oregon 43 (SW Macadam Blvd.). If you're heading south, that junction with Boones Ferry Road can be tricky — stay left on Terwilliger, following the signs to Lake Oswego, and then stay right, continuing to head to Lake Oswego.

A mathematician could go balmy calculating the possible combinations and permutations of itineraries within the park. Because of the backtracking necessary, it would be a frantic outing trying to cover all the routes in one session. Possible, of course, but, like all city hikes, the park lends itself to less compulsive explorations.

A suggested itinerary for first time visitors is to head south from Nature House and descend to Red Fox Bridge. Beyond it stay right at junctions and head west and north to High Bridge. At the junction beyond that span stay left, continue north and then curve south to the equestrian parking area and follow the road back to your car.

Trail Sign, Tryon Creek State Park

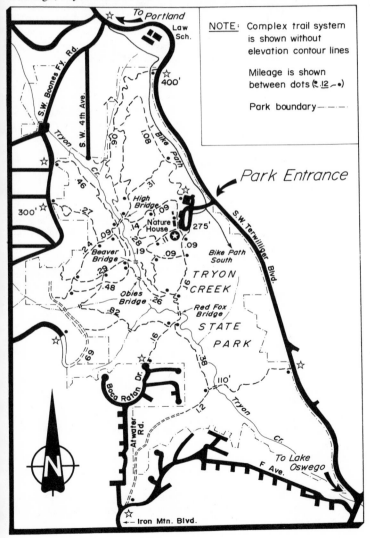

11 MARQUAM HILL — SAM JACKSON TRAILS

One day trip
Distance: 2.1 miles one way from Marquam Nature Park Center to Council Crest
Elevation gain: 820 feet from Marquam Nature Park Center to Council Crest
High point: 1,065 feet
Allow 1 to 1½ hours one way from Marquam Nature Park Center to Council Crest
Usually open all year
Topographic maps:
  U.S.G.S. Lake Oswego, Oreg.
  7.5'   1961
  U.S.G.S. Portland, Oreg.-Wash.
  7.5'   1961

The Marquam Hill-Sam Jackson Trails travel up canyons between Duniway Park and Council Crest. More precisely, the trail system is like the letter Y on its side with the stem (west) end the high point on Council Crest. The southeastern prong begins from SW Terwilliger Blvd. between SW Capitol Highway and Duniway Park and the northeastern one from just west of the park. From Council Crest you'll have one of the best panoramas in the Portland metropolitan area — west over the Tualatin Valley and east over the city to Mounts St. Helens, Ranier, Adams and Hood. People familiar with the Washington side of the Columbia Gorge will be able to identify Three Corner Rock and Table Mountain (No. 16). As you walk through the woods below

Council Crest you'll have glimpses of a few of the buildings of the Oregon Health Sciences University and the new Veterans Administration Hospital and pass many attractive homes.

To begin the hike from SW Terwilliger Blvd. (the trailhead shown on Map 2), follow Terwilliger 1.5 miles south from Duniway Park or 1.0 mile north from its junction with SW Capitol Highway to signs identifying the Marquam Trail and 40 Mile Loop. A parking turnout is a short distance south along Terwilliger. Perhaps because it's a new route, the first 0.5 mile or so can be muddy during or after wet weather. Where you come to a four-way junction at 1.0 mile keep straight and continue up to SW Marquam Hill Road. Turn left and walk along the street for several hundred feet to the signed resumption of the trail on the north shoulder. See Map 1 for the alignment of the Marquam Hill Trail from here to Council Crest.

If you want to begin from or establish a car shuttle to Council Crest, refer to a Portland street map.

To begin from the Marquam Nature Park Center, the lowest point, follow SW Sam Jackson Park Road about 0.2 mile west from its junction with Terwilliger Blvd. at Duniway Park. Where SW Sam Jackson Park Road curves sharply left stay straight on SW Marquam St. and park in the lot near the Center. This large, open sided building has engrossing displays illustrating the physical and cultural history of the area. Definitely take time to enjoy them.

There's a possible loop from this starting point. You can head up (or return) along the blocked, old dirt road that begins across SW Marquam St. from the west side of the Center. Farther on this leaf covered road narrows to a trail. Just beyond where you climb some steps come to a junction. The route to the left climbs to SW Marquam Hill Road and then descends from its other side to SW Terwilliger Blvd. (refer to Map 2). The route to the right above the steps connects with the northerly loop from the Center.

If you want to take this northerly route, walk from the Center up SW Marquam St., passing a couple of homes, to its end and the beginning of the Sam Jackson Trail.

From the junction of the Sam Jackson and Marquam Hill Trails at 0.4 mile continue uphill, crossing SW Sherwood Drive and SW Fairmont Blvd. Where you cross SW Greenway Ave. to a grassy slope look to its upper left corner for the resumption of a tread. Just below the summit a short connector goes to the lawn below the summit loop road. The main trail traverses along the northeast facing slope, which provides views not seen from the summit. On the north side come to a path heading to the crest, turn left onto it and meet the summit loop road just west of the restrooms.

View from near Council Crest

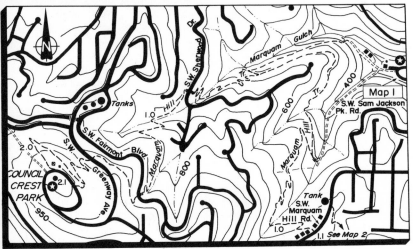

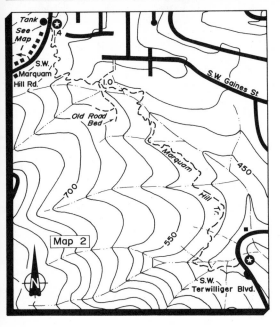

12　HOYT ARBORETUM

One day trip
Distance: 4.2 miles one way to Pittock
　　　　Mansion along Wildwood Trail
Elevation gain: 775 feet one way; loss
　　　　450 feet
High point: 940 feet
Allow 2½ hours one way
Usually open all year
Topographic map:
　U.S.G.S. Portland, Oreg.-Wash.
　7.5'　　1961

The Wildwood Trail is a 23 mile long route that traverses four contiguous city parks; Washington Park, Hoyt Arboretum, Macleay Park (No. 13) and Forest Park (No's. 14 and 15). Anywhere, a trail this long would be noteworthy but sprouting from the main branch are also dozens of side routes and most of these can be done as little loops. Nowhere are there as many options as in Hoyt Arboretum.

A suggested hike for first time visitors to this dense maze of trails is to follow the Wildwood Trail through the arboretum to the Pittock Mansion. This route takes you to a high ridge straddling the preserve where views extend over nearby terrain to landmarks as distant as Mounts Rainier, Adams and Hood then heads through the southeast corner of Washington Park past a view over the Japanese Gardens and continues into the concentrated plant-

ings of the arboretum. From the 2.8 mile point you can make a little inner loop along the Wildwood Trail (subsequently shortened to WWT) past more plantings or head directly to the mansion. The grounds, with their panoramic views, are always accessible to visitors and the mansion is open to the public at prescribed hours.

Because the trees in the arboretum bear identifying tags giving their common and scientific names, all hikes there can be food for the mind, as well as the body and soul. The Tree House (shown as Office and Restrooms on the map) on SW Fairview Blvd. contains both exhibits and literature on the arboretum. You're encouraged to drive to it before the hike or you could deviate from the itinerary described below and visit it as part of the walk.

The most efficient way to reach the official beginning of the WWT at the World Forestry Center is to take SW Canyon Road to the Zoo-OMSI exit and park in the northern end of the lot. The WWT begins from a large marker near the northeast corner of the main World Forestry Center Building.

If you want to establish a car shuttle, first drive both cars west on Burnside 1.2 miles from NW 23rd Ave. to NW Barnes Road, turn right and continue following signs to the mansion.

As the map shows, from the World Forestry Center you have several less circuitous routes than the WWT to reach the 1.0 mile point on the WWT. Along all of them you'll be traversing mostly grassy slopes where you'll have views south over the Zoo-OMSI complex to St. Thomas Moore Catholic Church. At 2.0 miles, a short distance beyond a view over the Japanese Gardens, come to a junction. Turn right, leaving the WWT, and descend to an even better overlook.

Return to the WWT, soon cross SW Cascade and Upper Cascade Drives and follow the Wildwood-Oak Tour Trails. Stay left where an unsigned use path goes right and then a bit farther turn right where the Wildwood and Oak Tour Trails diverge. Climb to SW Fairview Blvd., veer left and pick up the WWT on the west side. Keep right at all junctions as you descend and at 2.8 miles come to a bridge. The route to the left is the lower end of the inner loop of the WWT. Cross the bridge and wind up a short distance to a junction at an old road bed. The WWT to Macleay Park and the Pittock Mansion heads right here, crosses Burnside in 0.3 mile and climbs through lovely woods to the mansion.

To make the inner loop, stay left at the junction above the bridge, cross SW Fisher Lane and follow WWT signs. In 0.5 mile come to another bridge and the south end of the inner loop. If want to return directly to the Forestry Center from here stay right on the Hemlock Trail, climb to Fairview, cross it and descend to your starting point.

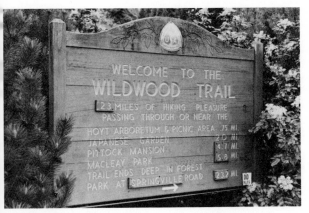

Sign at start of Wildwood Trail

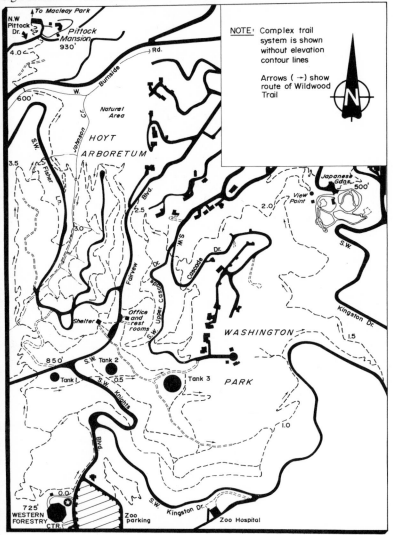

13 MACLEAY PARK

One day trip
Distance: 2.2 miles one way along the Wildwood Trail from Pittock Mansion to Forest Park Headquarters
Elevation gain: 100 feet; loss 950 feet along the Wildwood Trail from Pittock Mansion to Forest Park Headquarters
High point: 940 feet
Allow 1 hour along the Wildwood Trail from Pittock Mansion to Forest Park Headquarters
Usually open all year
Topographic map:
  U.S.G.S. Portland, Oreg.-Wash.
  7.5′   1961

Since the upper end of the Wildwood Trail through Macleay Park begins from the grand Pittock Mansion, it's appropriate that the route travels through an elegant woods of old growth conifers. When Donald Macleay deeded 104 acres to the City of Portland in 1897 he assumed the timber would be harvested but it wasn't and eventually a definite policy was adopted to preserve the trees. This stately forest affords a perfect transition between the calculated plantings of Hoyt Arboretum (No. 12) to the south and the more wild and woolly ambience of Forest Park (No's. 14 and 15) to the north.

From the mansion, the Wildwood Trail (subsequently shortened to WWT) descends to NW Cornell Road, which divides the park into Upper and Lower Macleay Parks, and continues down Balch Canyon beside a creek to Forest Park Headquarters under the Thurman St. bridge. There are five side trails and, if you're not using a car shuttle, you can take one of them as part of a loop on the return. The others are short enough that you could also easily explore them.

To reach the lower end of the trail at Forest Park

Headquarters drive on NW Upshur St. to its end one block west of NW 29th Ave. If you're approaching on NW Thurman St. note that you'll need to turn north onto 28th to reach Upshur because 29th is closed to cars. You also can walk down to Forest Park Headquarters from the east end of the Thurman St. bridge.

If you want to begin from NW Cornell Road, the easiest approach for most drivers is to head west on NW Lovejoy St. At about the equivalent of 26th the main route curves right and you'll be on Cornell automatically. (Note that Cornell is scheduled to be closed for repairs through mid-October, 1986.)

To reach the upper end of the trail at Pittock Mansion take Burnside west from NW 23rd Ave. for 1.2 miles to NW Barnes Road, turn right and continue following signs to Pittock Mansion. Before or after the hike walk past the mansion to enjoy the groomed grounds and the panorama over Portland and considerably beyond. The mansion is open at prescribed hours and a small entrance fee is charged.

You might have noticed trails heading off from both sides of Burnside 0.1 mile before Barnes Road. These are sections of the WWT between Hoyt Arboretum and Macleay Park (see No. 12 for details).

To follow the WWT through Macleay Park take the route from the northwest corner of the parking lot. At the first junction you have three options: you can turn left and take Upper Macleay Trail to Cornell; you can turn right and follow a high route to NW Macleay Blvd. and return to the WWT along a lower, parallel route; or you can stay straight on the WWT. If you opt to continue on the WWT (with or without the side loop to NW Macleay Blvd.), it's recommended you stay left on the WWT at the junction of the Cumberland Trail. Those not doing the hike as a car shuttle can then make a return loop from Lower Macleay Park along the Tunnel and Cumberland Trails. The Upper Macleay Trail and WWT rejoin just above where you cross Cornell.

Beyond the east side of the stone marker on Cornell head west and then wind down into Balch Canyon. The stone ruins you pass midway down the canyon are of a shelter built by CCC crews. Just beyond the building come to a junction. The WWT angles left here and begins its traverse through Forest Park. Stay straight (right) and after 130 yards come to the junction of the Tunnel Trail. The Lower Macleay Trail continues for another 0.5 mile beside the creek to Forest Park Headquarters.

To make the suggested return loop, turn onto the Tunnel Trail and climb to Cornell. Turn left and walk along it for 150 yards to the resumption of the trail across Cornell on the far side of a turnout. Climb to a junction with the Cumberland Trail. The route left goes to NW Cumberland and the one right soon meets the WWT.

Balch Canyon

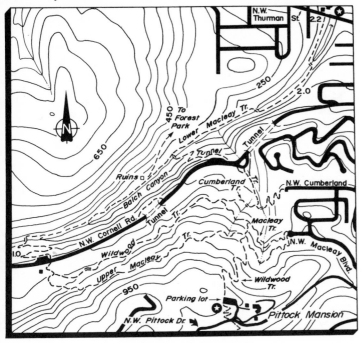

14 FOREST PARK: BALCH CANYON to ROCKING CHAIR DAM

One day trip
Distance: 6.8 miles one way along the Wildwood Trail
Elevation gain: 900 feet along the Wildwood Trail, loss 400 feet
High point: 850 feet along the Wildwood Trail
Allow 4 to 4½ hours one way along the Wildwood Trail
Usually open all year
Topographic maps:
U.S.G.S Linnton, Oreg.
7.5′   1961
U.S.G.S. Portland, Oreg.-Wash.
7.5′   1961

Because only about 6.0 miles of the 23 mile long Wildwood Trail (subsequently referred to as the WWT) are used meandering past the scenic delights of Hoyt Arboretum (No. 12) and Macleay Park (No. 13), this leaves about 17 miles for the traverse along the wooded slopes of Forest Park, at 5,000 plus acres one of the largest of urban preserves. Diverging from this main route are many side trails, most of which can be combined into loops back to the WWT. Plus, several of these spurs go to roads, so hikers have options where they can begin (and end, if they want to establish car shuttles). Note that, currently, NW Leif Erikson Drive is closed to vehicular travel. From a peace and quiet perspective, this policy, in effect, about doubles the width of Forest Park and more than compensates for preventing access by car to a few side trails.

To reach Forest Park Headquarters and the south end of the WWT through Forest Park drive on NW Upshur St. to its end one block west of NW 29th Ave. If you're approaching on NW Thurman St. note that you'll need to turn north onto 28th to reach

Upshur because 29th is not open to vehicles. You also can walk down to Forest park Headquarters from the east end of the Thurman St. bridge.

Walk up beside the creek flowing through Balch Canyon for 0.7 mile to the junction of the WWT on your right just before the picturesque ruins of a stone shelter. Persistent vandalism finally defeated attempts to maintain this facility. Destruction of a less malicious, but considerably more grandiose, variety almost occurred in 1905 when a Colorado man wanted to sluice away Balch Canyon to fill what was then Guilds Lake.

Turn right onto the WWT, climb out of Balch Canyon and where you come to a three-way junction above Holman Park keep straight. All of the WWT and its spurs are impeccably signed and little metal tags on trees methodically give mileages along the WWT from the Forestry Center. Pass the Aspen Trail on your right, a short connector to NW Aspen St., and after traveling in and out of three side canyons come to the Birch Trail on your left, the most southerly of the several connectors to NW 53rd Dr., which you can reach by following NW Cornell Road (refer to No. 13) to the first road on your right beyond (north of) the Audubon Bird Sanctuary. Farther on walk beside the remains of a canal that was constructed in 1905 to carry water to the Lewis and Clark Exposition.

At 3.0 miles come to the junction of the Wild Cherry Trail that extends from 53rd to Leif Erikson Drive. Farther on cross the Dogwood Trail that begins from 53rd just a couple hundred feet north of the Wild Cherry Trial and also continues down to Leif Erikson Dr. The WWT through Forest Park is mostly level but you can exercise climbing and descending muscles by following these side routes. About 0.6 mile farther along the WWT skirt just yards below 53rd and 0.2 mile farther pass Alder Trail, the last access to Leif Erikson Dr. before Rocking Chair Dam.

Continue in and out of side canyons to Forest Lane, an unpaved road with a good surface that connects to 53rd about 0.8 mile northwest of the beginning of the Wild Cherry and Dogwood Trails. You can cross Forest Lane and continue along the WWT or you can turn right, follow down the open swath from the road's end to the beginning of a Nature Trail. It winds down past a picnic shelter to a junction where one route continues descending to Rocking Chair Dam and a short connector goes up to the WWT. From Forest Lane the WWT drops to the connector to the Nature Trail and then climbs to the junction of the Chestnut Trail, which goes down the other side of the little canyon to Rocking Chair Dam. The dam, now in disrepair, was built to create a reservoir for fire fighting. Refer to No. 15 for a description of the remainder of the WWT.

Trailside shelter

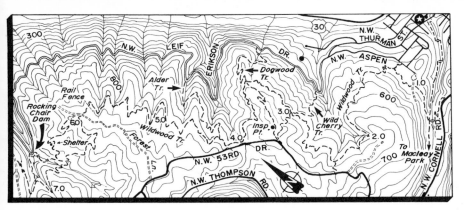

15 FOREST PARK: ROCKING CHAIR DAM to NW SPRINGVILLE ROAD

One day trip
Distance: 11.5 miles one way along the Wildwood Trail
Elevation gain: 300 feet one way along the Wildwood Trail; loss 200 feet
High point: 900 feet
Allow 6 to 7 hours one way along the Wildwood Trail
Usually open all year
Topographic maps:
  U.S.G.S. Linnton, Oreg.
  7.5'   1961
  U.S.G.S. Portland, Oreg.-Wash.
  7.5'   1961

Prior to the mid-1960's no formal trails existed in Forest Park north of Rocking Chair Dam with the exception of the Hardesty Trail that the Mazamas built near what is now Fire Lane 7 south of NW Springville Road. But the concentrated construction that improved established routes in the southern portion of the park (see No. 14) also included extending the Wildwood Trail (subsequently shortened to WWT) to NW Saltzman Road and building the Maple Loop off of it. In 1980 the final 7.6 miles of the WWT was completed from NW Saltzman to NW Springville Roads.

Because Leif Erikson Drive is currently closed to vehicles (a policy most park visitors would applaud), there's no access by car to Rocking Chair Dam. However, for mapping purposes, the dam's location about midway through Forest Park makes it a good division point. So, refer to No. 14 for descriptions of accesses from the south. That previous write-up ended at the 7.2 mile point at the junction of the Chestnut Trail down to Rocking Chair Dam. (Note that the mileage figures will continue from 7.2, not 0.0, beyond this junction.)

Beyond the Chestnut Trail come to a new alignment of the WWT, which should be open later in 1986, that saves some elevation gain and distance. The original route will remain open so there will be yet another possible little side loop. Near the northerly junction of the old and new WWT come to the Maple Trail. This 4.2 mile side loop descends, crosses and then travels below Leif Erikson Dr. It crosses NW Saltzman Road, which connects to NW St. Helens Road, and then meets Erikson north from where Erikson and Saltzman intersect. The route heads right on Erikson for 0.2 mile and then follows a trail up a canyon past an enclosed reservoir to the WWT.

Particularly if you're hiking from late fall through early spring when the deciduous trees are leafless, you'll note that the farther north you head from Rocking Chair Dam the more the forest is composed of them, rather than coniferous trees. The slopes near the Willamette River were logged by the first settlers in the mid-1800's. As demand increased, harvesting became more extensive and most of the northern portion of Forst Park has been logged several times. Also, in addition to slash burning, numerous small fires and two extensive ones, the Bonny Slope in 1920 and the Linnton in 1951, have devastated the area over the decades. High winds, most notably in the Columbus Day Storm of 1962, have also destroyed many conifers and created room for the initially faster growing deciduous trees.

At a second powerline cut along the WWT at 10.5 miles come to a view toward Rivergate, Vancouver Lake and the Columbia River. Traverse downhill for a short distance to Saltzman Road about 0.6 mile above its junction with Leif Erikson Dr. Note that Saltzman is gated a short distance below Skyline and also where it meets Erikson.

The final 7.6 miles of the WWT beyond Saltzman traverses convoluted terrain with many little side canyons. In order to maintain a mostly level grade the route is very sinuous. Among the dominant alders and maples and a few conifers you'ss spot some madrone trees. They have big, shiny, laurel like leaves and as summer growth begins the bark peels leaving smooth trunks and limbs that eventually turn to a terra cotta. Springville is also gated just below Skyline so, if you're establishing a shuttle, you'll need to leave one car on Skyline and hike along Springville for the 0.8 mile to or from the WWT.

Almost completed early in 1986 is the 2.1 mile connector between Springville and NW Germantown Roads.

Forest Park

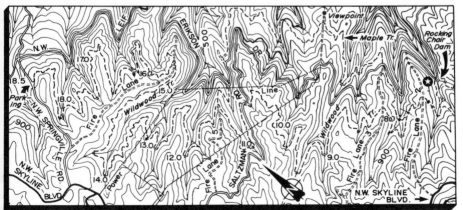

Loowit Falls, Eagle Creek Canyon

Munra Point and Table Mountain

Upper Multnomah Creek

columbia gorge

The Columbia Gorge is in Portland's backyard and traveling below its uncounted waterfalls, traversing stream filled, steep walled canyons, crossing open, wildflower splashed or deeply wooded slopes and climbing narrow ridges past massive rock outcroppings to viewpoints are almost 200 miles of trails. These routes afford every degree of difficulty from ambles to super loops of 20 miles with 5,000 feet of elevation gain and every foot of every route is a visual treat. Three months before the trails in the high country are snow free the Gorge routes are fresh with the year's new life. Later in the fall, when the higher routes are again snow covered, those leaves turn color and the Gorge puts on its second major show. Summer in the Gorge is fine, too — it's just not as flashy as spring and fall. Unless winter is exceptionally severe, the lowest elevation trails can be hiked throughout the year. A bonus for taking them in winter is that you'll have views that will be blocked when the trees have leafed.

No area has benefitted more from the renaissance of trail building from the late 1960's through the very early 1980's than the Gorge. With three major exceptions, most of this construction was the reopening of long abandoned routes. In addition to Forest Service crews, hikers can thank members of the Mazamas, Sierra Club, Trails Club and Boy Scouts and other volunteers for this work. The last of these formerly impassable routes to be opened was the Moffett Creek Trail (No. 24). For several years small crews have been nibbling away at reopening Bell Creek Way that once connected the Franklin Ridge and Horsetail Creek Trails between the 3,200 and 2,800 foot levels. A recalcitrant area of colossal blowdown and the current lack of funds make it problematical when it will be hikeable again.

Two of those exceptions to the general rule of trails being reopened, rather then built new, are the realignments of the northernmost portion of the Pacific Crest Trail in Oregon (see No. 21) and considerably more of the southernmost part of the PCT in Washington (see No. 16). The third exception is the Gorge Trail (No's. 17 through 21) that currently extends from Bridal Veil to the Columbia Gorge Work Center east of Cascade Locks. For this low elevation traverse, many new sections of tread were built to connect already existing routes.

Compared to other areas, the outdoor hazards in the Pacific Northwest are benign. And, aside from the risks inherent on any hike, two of the three nuisances you have to contend with for the 50 hikes described in this guide are confined to the Gorge: poison oak and ticks. (The third is mosquitoes but the places they thrive in the Gorge, especially the Benson Plateau, aren't visited by any of these trails. However, it's probably a good idea to put a can of repellent in your pack for all hikes from spring through late summer.) Particularly in spring, check your clothing carefully for ticks when you stop for lunch. Check again before getting into your car and then examine your whole body very carefully when you arrive home. Fortunately, ticks aren't usually in a hurry to dig in so you have some time to find them before they start using you for a lunch counter. If one has begun to burrow in you should be able to remove it with tweezers, using a slow, steady and gentle pull. Be sure all of the critter has been removed. Some people may have a red area around the bite for a few days. If you stay on the trail and recognize what poison oak looks like so you don't accidentally come into contact with it, you shouldn't have any problems. As with ticks, you won't even see it on many hikes. If you have spotted some you should take an especially thorough shower. Also, wash your hiking clothes as soon as possible because you can pick up the noxious oils from touching clothing, boots, packs, etc. that have come in contact with the plant. And don't forget about your dog — if he's been exploring off the trail be circumspect about petting or hugging him.

Except for two hikes that come in high from the south (No's. 27 and 28), all the Gorge routes are accessible from I-84 — or Washington 14 for Table Mountain (No. 16). Watch weather forecasts when you plan hikes from late fall through early spring because Gorge weather can become extremely nasty and hazardous. Of the hikes on the Oregon side only the Powerline Access Trail (No. 26) is not connected with other routes. If you want to add onto the hikes described here you can refer to *Forest Trails of the Columbia Gorge*, the recreation map for the area prepared by the US Forest Service, or *35 Hiking Trails — Columbia River Gorge* by Don and Roberta Lowe.

16 TABLE MOUNTAIN

One day trip
Distance: 7.2 miles one way
Elevation gain: 3,650 feet; loss 250 feet
Allow 4½ to 5½ hours one way
Usually open April through mid December
High point: 3,417 feet
Topographic map:
  U.S.G.S. Bonneville Dam, Wash.-Oreg.
  7.5'   1979

Late in 1984 work was completed on the new alignment of the southernmost 18.6 miles of the Pacific Crest Trail in Washington. This segment passes just east of Three Corner Rock, eventually traverses the western and southern flanks of Table Mountain and ends at Washington 14 just 100 yards west of the Bridge of the Gods. Now Table Mountain, long a favorite conditioning hike, is accessible along a trail, not a road. Although a 14 plus mile round trip hike is a respectable outing, regardless of the elevation gain, what makes the climb of Table Mountain such a mettle tester is that half of its considerable uphill is gained in the last 1.4 miles. The views are as impressive as the grade and from the summit and the open slopes below it they extend over the Columbia River and landmarks on the Oregon side from Larch Mountain to Mt. Defiance (No. 27) and directly down onto Bonneville Dam. Mt. Hood rises behind the green walls of the Gorge and to the north are Mounts St. Helens, Rainier and Adams. Note that the uppermost portions of the hike are faint and a few sections of the steep pitches are rubbly.

Drive on Washington 14 for 0.6 mile east of the 40 mile post or 1.0 mile west of the Bridge of the Gods to a turnout with historical markers on the south side of the highway at Fort Rains. Because the PCT parallels Washington 14 between the Bridge of the Gods and Fort Rains, you might as well begin from the latter and save 1.0 mile of hiking.

Cross the highway, walk a hundred or so feet up the paved road to a gate and turn left onto the PCT. Meander up through woods for 2.2 miles to a gravel road. Here would have been a better place to begin except this road — and the popular, shorter route from Greenleaf Slough — traverse private property. From the other side of the road walk down an old roadbed above Gillette Lake. Several hundred feet beyond it cross a good sized stream on a bridge. Resume climbing to a pipeline access road, turn left and after 200 feet come to the resumption of the trail. Farther on descend in one switchback to another big stream and a bridge. Wind up to a grassy, rocky ledge at 3.8 miles. Walk through a pocket of alder and maple, wind up in several switchbacks, cross over the nose of a ridge and begin travelling above a dirt road. At 5.0 miles cross it, make a little loop off its west side and meet it a second time.

Although you can cross the road and continue along the PCT, you'll get more variety for your effort by following the road. At 5.5 miles cross a stream, a good place for a snack stop, and continue in the same direction for a couple hundred feet to a junction. The route up to the right crosses the PCT and continues climbing steeply as part of the easterly loop on Table Mountain. However, to take the recommended route, turn left and come to a second creek, the last source of water on the climb. After fording it veer left to locate the trail, wind up and soon after you cross the PCT begin that promised very steep grade.

Where you come to the flat area on the west end of the summit ridge walk north toward a wall of woods, follow a path to the left and head to the open area with those views of the Washington peaks. To complete the loop along its eastern leg, which is 0.5 mile shorter, and therefore steeper, retrace your route to the woods and have easy cross-country to the grassy south face. Continue east along the summit ridge to a faint path angling off down to the right. (Be careful if you explore beyond the junction as the cliff face is undercut.) Where the path down becomes faint head south and then southeast to a short rocky swath. At its bottom come to a trail that is well defined for the remainder of the descent. The awesome sheer slope to the east is what's left after a great portion of Table Mountain and Greenleaf Peak slid away, temporarily blocking the Columbia River and earning a place in Indian lore.

Table Mountain

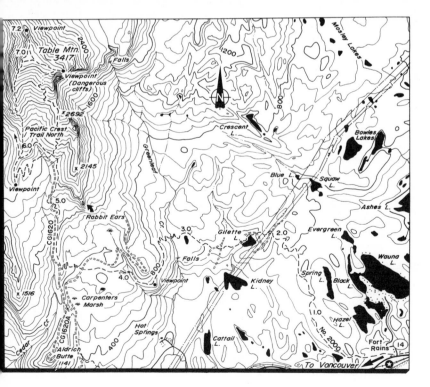

17 GORGE TRAIL: BRIDAL VEIL to MULTNOMAH FALLS

One day trip
Distance: 8 miles one way
Elevation gain: 2,350 feet; loss 250 feet
High point: 2,100 feet
Allow 5 hours one way
Usually open March through December
Topographic map:
 U.S.G.S. Bridal Veil, Wash.-Oreg.
 15′   1954

Around the mid 1970's work began on a low elevation route along the Oregon side of the Columbia Gorge. Existing treads were to be connected by new routes or the reopening of long abandoned ones. Originally, the Gorge Trail No. 400 (No's. 17 through 21) was to have extended from Wahkeena Creek east to Wyeth but the section from Bridal Veil over Angels Rest to Wahkeena Creek, though a bit higher than the originators had envisioned, was too good to leave out. And the State of Oregon has just begun construction of a trail that will ultimately extend from Bridal Veil west to the Sandy River. All sections are perfect for car shuttles, can be made longer, or with the exception of No. 21, shorter.

Drive east on I-84 to the Bridal Veil Exit 28 and climb for 0.4 mile to the parking area between the exit road and its junction with the Columbia River Scenic Highway. (There's no Bridal Veil Exit for westbound traffic, so drivers coming from the east will need to take the Ainsworth Park Exit 35 and continue west along the Scenic Highway for 7.0 miles.) For those establishing a shuttle, Multnomah Falls is 3.1 miles east along the Scenic Highway from the Bridal Veil Exit.

The west end of the Gorge Trail, which may not be signed, begins across the Scenic Highway from the parking area and traverses up a bank. Climb gradually through woods, switchback twice and then cross a talus slope where you can see across the Columbia River to the cliffs of Cape Horn. Several yards beyond the rocks keep left where an abandoned route heads to the right and enter a side canyon. Pass a spur to a view of Coopey Falls and soon cross Coopey Creek on a bridge. Continue up in switchbacks and traverses, farther on alternating between the north and south sides of a ridge, to an open rocky area at 1.8 miles. Travel through brushy vegetation, switchback and then resume hiking on a tread of slabs to an unsigned junction on a narrow ridge top. To reach the exceptional view from Angels Rest keep straight (left).

To continue along the Gorge Trail, turn right on the main route at the narrow crest, walk along its spine and re-enter woods. Follow an erratic grade and at 2.8 miles cross a small stream and pass a picnic area. At 3.6 miles pass the signed Primrose Way Trail (not shown on map) that climbs streeply to Devils Rest. Near 3.7 miles begin descending in six long switchbacks then climb slightly to Wahkeena Creek and travel near it for a few hundred feet to Wahkeena Spring.

Come to a junction about 300 feet beyond the spring. If you want to head directly down beside Wahkeena Creek to the Scenic Highway or to follow the lower Perdition Trail No. 421 to Multnomah Falls, turn left. But if you intend to take the high route to Multnomah Creek or the scenic easterly loop along Trail No. 419 that rejoins the Wahkeena Trail a short distance above Fairy Falls, stay right. You'll reach the top of the Vista Point Trail No. 419 on your left after 0.4 mile of uphill. The junction of the 2.0 mile route to Devils Rest is on your right 75 feet farther along Trail No. 420. Soon begin descending and eventually come to the junction of Trail No. 441 at Multnomah Creek. Turn left and follow beside the stream, which with its many cascades, falls and pools is among the most scenic in the Gorge. Come to the junction of the east end of the Perdition Trail just before the bridge over Multnomah Creek. Stay right, cross the flow to a paved tread and after a brief climb begin switchbacking down to the lodge at Multnomah Falls, passing the continuation of the Gorge Trail on the last turn at 7.7 miles.

Trail Map at Wahkeena Creek

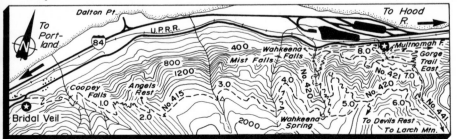

18 GORGE TRAIL: MULTNOMAH FALLS to AINSWORTH INTERCHANGE

One day trip
Distance: 6 miles one way
Elevation gain: 800 feet; loss 300 feet
High point: 500 feet
Allow 3 to 3½ hours one way
Usually open February through December
Topographic map:
U.S.G.S. Bridal Veil, Wash.-Oreg.
15′   1954

In addition to visiting popular Multnomah and Pony Tail Falls, the section of the Gorge Trail from Multnomah Creek to east of Ainsworth Park passes short routes to three more waterfalls. Like the other segments of the Gorge Trail (No's. 17 through 21), this portion is ideal for a car shuttle and can be made shorter or considerably longer.

Proceed on I-84 to the Multnomah Falls Exit 31 and take the pedestrian tunnel under the railroad tracks. If you're doing the hike as a shuttle, first drive both cars on I-84 to the Ainsworth Park Exit 35 and park one vehicle along the south side of the interchange complex near where an obvious, but possibly unsigned, path switchbacks down a low, grassy bank. Drive the second car west along the Scenic Highway or I-84 back to Multnomah Falls.

Follow the paved trail that heads from the east side of the lodge up to the bridge, go out of the canyon and traverse to the first switchback at the junction of the unpaved Ak-Wanee Trail. Stay straight and continue traversing for 0.5 mile to a swath of moss covered rocks. Near the east end look for the faint tread of the Elevator Shaft (No. 22)that switchbacks upslope. Round the edge of the mossy rocks and in a couple hundred feet come to a slide area. Look for the resumption of the tread across the rubble and easily pick your way to it.

Traverse gradually uphill to an unsigned fork at 2.1 miles. You're encouraged to take the abandoned spur on your right 0.2 mile to its end at the base of a high rock wall where two whispy waterfalls float down the face. Descend to the Scenic Highway along the main trail and walk beside the road for several yards to the resumption of the tread. Climb noticeably for a short distance and then again follow a gradual grade. After 0.2 mile pass beneath remnants of an old, man made rock wall and several yards farther come to the Oneonta Creek Trail.

Stay right, traverse up, curve into the canyon holding Oneonta Creek and watch for the signed junction of the Horsetail Falls Trail No. 438. If you want to make the 0.8 mile side trip to the view of Triple Falls, stay straight. To continue on the Gorge Trail, descend to the bridge across Oneonta Creek, wind up in several short switchbacks and traverse out of the canyon. Take either fork at a junction, traverse and walk through the cavern behind Pony Tail Falls. Farther on begin descending and at the third switchback keep straight (right) on the Gorge Trail.

The tall wooden fence you'll pass at 4.5 miles was built in the early 1920's to keep snow from avalanching onto the road and railroad tracks because, then, there was no forest of big trees. Just beyond the barricade come to the junction of an optional side loop down to the Scenic Highway. The loop resumes from the west side of a restroom building a short distance east along the road. The main trail stays high and continues traversing. About 0.4 mile beyond where the easterly portion of the side loop rejoins the main trail come to the possibly unsigned junction of a path that winds down to Ainsworth Campground.

Stay right and after 0.2 mile meet an obvious, but unmarked, cross-path, the east end of the infamous Mystery Trail. It climbs steeply and traverses exposed slopes to the rim of the Gorge and follows the Horsetail Creek and then Rock of Ages Ridge Trails down to near Pony Tail Falls. Following the route for its initial 0.3 mile is fun but don't go beyond the rocky stream bed as the slope becomes steep and unstable. The remaining 0.4 mile of the Gorge Trail continues through pleasing woods lush with sword ferns along one section and then passes through a small blackberry patch before making four little switchbacks down to the highway. The Gorge Trail resumes 0.7 mile to the east at Dodson.

Bridge over Oneonta Creek

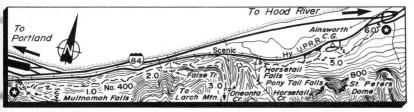

19 GORGE TRAIL: DODSON to TANNER CREEK

One day trip
Distance: 5.4 miles one way
Elevation gain: 1,000 feet; loss 200 feet
High point: 800 feet
Allow 3 hours one way
Usually open mid February through
December
Topographic maps:
  U.S.G.S. Bonneville Dam, Oreg.-Wash.
  15'   1957
  U.S.G.S Bridal Veil, Wash.-Oreg.
  15'   1954

Every section of the Gorge Trail (No's. 17 through 21) passes waterfalls and the route between Dodson and Tanner Creek goes to the base of one of the loveliest, Lower Elowah Falls. A highly recommended visit to the upper falls follows a 0.7 mile spur that traverses high on the sheer west wall of McCord Creek canyon. For a shorter hike, you can begin or end at Yeon State Park near the midway point. As with all sections of the Gorge Trail, this one is perfect for a car shuttle.

Drive on I-84 to the Ainsworth Park Exit 35. At the end of the exit turn left, following the sign to Dodson, and after 150 feet turn right onto the signed frontage road — don't rejoin the freeway. Follow the frontage road for 0.5 mile to McLoughlin Parkway, the road to Bonneville School. Turn right onto it and travel 0.1 mile to a dirt road blocked by two cement stanchions on your left just beyond the junction of Gwen Avenue and before the fence around the school yard. If you intend to begin from Yeon State Park, continue along the frontage road for another 1.7 miles to a large parking area on your right just before the road rejoins I-84. To establish a shuttle at the easterly end, drive both cars along I-84 to the Bonneville Dam Exit 40. At the end of the exit turn right, come to a T-junction and park off the road.

From near Bonneville School walk into woods along the old road blocked by those posts. Keep left at a fork, as indicated by a sign, eventually begin travelling on a trail and continue gently uphill. Cross two streams, which after heavy rains can be surprisingly voluminous. However, they're no problem to ford. Continue gradually climbing then descend slightly and cross another old road. Wind among small alders and maples and then travel along a grass covered roadbed. At a wash look up for a good view of impressive rock formations along the Gorge wall. On the east side of a bridge at 1.6 miles meet the junction of the trail up to Nesmith Point (see No's. 23 and 24) and stay left (downhill). Traverse along a rocky slope, soon cross a stream and wind down in good looking woods to a junction above the parking area for Yeon State Park.

To continue along the Gorge Trail, turn right, walk through a corridor of deciduous trees to a forest of especially stately evergreens. Climb a bit to the possibly unsigned junction of the spur that ends at creek level just beyond Upper Elowah Falls. The Gorge Trail continues east, traversing a rocky slope populated with a few conies and then winds down. Walk along the canyon to near the base of Lower Elowah Falls and cross McCord Creek on a bridge. The immense boulder you skirt used to be a viewpoint considerably higher on the canyon wall but slid to its less lofty position in the mid 1960's. Maintaining this short section up from the creek had always been a problem for trail crews and after that big one came down the route was abandoned for over a decade. You'll pass the original trail to the former overlook as you traverse out of the canyon.

Farther on come to an open area at a former gravel dump where you can see Beacon Rock and Hamilton Mountain on the Washington side. Continue east across the open area to the resumption of a proper trail. Cross two scree slopes of moss covered rocks and at 4.1 miles ford Moffett Creek. About 200 feet beyond the stream pass the unsigned 1.2 mile use path that climbs steeply to Munra Point. Farther on begin travelling on an overgrown road, keeping left where forks head uphill, then resume hiking on a trail for the final distance to Tanner Creek and cross it on one of those charming bridges that graced the original Columbia River Highway.

Lower Elowah Falls

20 GORGE TRAIL: TANNER CREEK to CASCADE LOCKS

One day trip
Distance: 5 miles one way
Elevation gain: 700 feet; loss 300 feet
High point: 600 feet
Allow 3 hours one way
Usually open mid February through
December
Topographic map:
U.S.G.S. Bonneville Dam, Oreg.-Wash.
15'   1957

Among the benefits of the development of the low elevation Gorge Trail (No's. 17 through 21) is the terrain opened up by the construction of treads to connect already existing routes. As with the previous segment from Dodson to Tanner Creek, the western and easternmost portions from Tanner Creek to Cascade Locks are brand new. The middle stretch is along a considerably older route, a section of the original Columbia River Highway build 70 years ago. This portion of the Gorge Trail, like the others, is perfect for a car shuttle and can be made shorter or longer.

Proceed on I-84 to the Bonneville Dam Exit 40, turn right at the end of the exit and then after several yards come to a T-junction and park off the road. To establish a shuttle, first drive both cars to the Cascade Locks Exit 44, follow the approach to the Bridge of the Gods and leave one car in the little park enclosed by the road. If you want to begin or end at the midway point, take I-84 to the Eagle Creek Park Exit 41 (there's no westbound exit), turn right and park in front of the stone restroom building.

From the westerly trailhead near Tanner Creek climb the bank on the south side of the T-junction in one short switchback and walk along a catwalk over a pipe. Traverse above an old flume, which once supplied water to the fish hatchery at Bonneville Dam, and make three switchbacks, separated by long traverses, to a clearing. Continue in the same direction you were heading for a couple hundred feet to a road. Turn left and follow it 0.2 mile to unpaved Tanner Road that begins from the T-junction where you parked your car (see No. 24). (If you're hiking from east to west, beyond Tanner Road stay right at all forks along the secondary road and head into the clearing. As the faint road curves left at the north side of the clearing stay straight and go between an old log on the left and a big root system on the right. The obvious tread begins several yards beyond them and heads down to the northwest.)

Turn left on Tanner Road and follow it 0.2 mile to a switchback and a marker on your right identifying Trail No. 402B. After 0.5 mile along this route come to the junction of the 0.8 mile spur that switchbacks up to Wauna Viewpoint with its exceptional perspective down onto Bonneville Dam and a view northeast to Mt. Adams. The main trail descends in two sets of switchbacks, curves into Eagle Creek canyon, makes one more turn and comes to a junction. This is the upper end of a nature loop so you can take either branch, although the left one is the more frequently used. Cross the suspension bridge over Eagle Creek, turn left onto the road then curve right at the stone restroom and follow the road that goes to the campground for about 75 yards to a sign on your left identifying the route to Cascade Locks. Wind up to the edge of a bluff, follow along the fence to the northeast end of the campground and the junction of the 0.3 mile spur trail to Buck Point.

Keep straight (left), descend to a large clearing, angle across it to the southeast and then at the trees veer left onto a rubble strewn section of the old Columbia River Highway. Pass the junction of the Ruckel Creek Trail (see No. 25) and continue along the roadbed, now soft underfoot with moss, for 0.8 mile to the resumption of a trail. Farther on come to an open slope where you can see the Bridge of the Gods, re-enter woods and wind through an exotic scene of vegetation draped rock outcroppings. Cross a narrow road, continue in woods for 0.1 mile to more open slopes and travel along them until you meet a road. The Gorge Trail continues directly across this road.

To reach Cascade Locks, turn left and walk down the road for 100 feet to a paved one. Stay straight (left) and after 75 feet come under an I-84 overpass. Veer left onto a signed trail, stay left at an unsigned fork and after 75 yards come to the little park near the bridge.

SAMUEL C. LANCASTER
1864 - 1941
CHIEF ENGINEER
SCENIC COLUMBIA RIVER HIGHWAY 1913 - 1915

PIONEER BUILDER OF HARD-SURFACE ROADS. HIS GENIUS OVERCAME TREMENDOUS OBSTACLES, EXTENDING AND REPLACING THE EARLY TRAIL THROUGH THE COLUMBIA RIVER GORGE WITH A HIGHWAY OF POETRY AND DRAMA SO THAT MILLIONS COULD ENJOY GOD'S SPECTACULAR CREATIONS.

21 GORGE TRAIL: CASCADE LOCKS to the COLUMBIA GORGE WORK CENTER

One day trip
Distance: 5.6 miles one way
Elevation gain: 1,200 feet; loss 200 feet
High point: 1,000 feet
Allow 3 hours one way
Usually open late February through mid
  December
Topographic map:
  U.S.G.S. Bonneville Dam, Oreg.-Wash.
  15'   1957

As of late 1985, the low elevation Gorge Trail (No's 17 through 21) is completed as far east as Herman Camp. Volunteers have built short portions of tread beyond the Camp and west from Wyeth but, as far as entry and exit points are concerned, the Gorge Trail's eastern end currently is at the Columbia Gorge Work Center. The initial 3.8 miles east from Cascade Locks follows the Pacific Crest Trail and special features include a cluster of uncommon rock pinnacles and an exceptionally large salamander population. Unlike the other four units, this segment has no intermediary access point but, like them, is perfect for a car shuttle. Begin with adequate water.

Drive on I-84 to the Cascade Locks Exit 44. If you're establishing a shuttle, continue with both cars east through town for 1.0 mile to a sign pointing left to Industrial Park and Airport. Turn left, after 2.2 miles cross over I-84 and turn left. Three-tenths mile farther turn right into the Columbia Gorge Work Center. Stay left on the road up to the new campground and trailhead and continue to the northwesternmost corner. With the other car retrace your route to the west end of Cascade Locks, turn left onto the approach to the Bridge of the Gods and go into the little park enclosed by the curve of the road.

From the exit of the park cross the approach road, walk 100 yards along a trail and meet another road under I-84. Turn right and in 75 feet meet a dirt road, stay straight and follow it for 100 feet to a sign pointing left to the the PCT. (For a description of the section of the Gorge Trail that heads west to Eagle Creek see No. 20.) Initially head south along the PCT and then curve east. At 0.9 mile come to a narrow dirt road, turn right and follow it about 75 feet to the resumption of the trail on your left. Watch for those salamanders, both so you can enjoy them and, more importantly, so you don't inadvertently squish one. Where you come to a wider dirt road look back about 20 feet for a faint path heading to the southwest. This is the beginning of the demanding Rudolph Spur Trail (No. 25).

On the east side of the road cross a bridge over Dry Creek, continue traversing through woods and then come to a scree slope where the view extends across the Columbia River to Stevenson and Table Mountain (No. 16). Re-enter woods and come to those unique pinnacles. A bit beyond them at a creek look upstream for a tall waterfall. Cross a larger scree slope with mossy rocks where you may hear (and see) some conies, a short distance farther traverse a considerably smaller rocky area where you can look across the canyon to a section of the trail you'll soon be on. Shortly after re-entering woods come to a junction.

Stay left, leaving the PCT, and descend to a bridge, which can be very slippery when wet. One-tenth mile beyond the span stay straight (left) where a path heads off to the right and 0.2 mile farther come to a signed junction. (When completed, the Gorge Trail will follow the route to the right (east) here, traverse to a road and follow it 0.5 mile to Herman Camp and the beginning of the Gorton Creek Trail. The Gorge Trail will head to the northeast here from Herman Camp.) For now, though, stay straight (left) descend to a narrow powerline access road, cross it and wind down. Where you come to a junction at a switchback stay right.

66

Dry Creek Falls

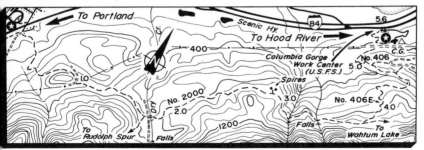

22   ELEVATOR SHAFT

One day trip
Distance: 1.8 miles one way
Elevation gain: 1,250 feet; loss 200 feet
High point: 1,260 feet
Allow 1½ hours one way
Usually open February through December
Topographic map:
  U.S.G.S. Bridal Veil, Wash.-Oreg.
  15'   1954

The Elevator Shaft, also known as the Fire Escape, is an immense talus slope on the face of the Gorge about 0.5 mile east of Multnomah Falls. A long abandoned path corkscrews up the moss covered rocks to the rim and then heads to a viewpoint above Multnomah Creek. Experienced hikers familiar with the area could make a loop by heading through a portion of Multnomah Basin and returning along the Multnomah Creek Trail No. 441.

Be warned that a few short sections on the talus slope are very brushy. Less tolerable is the poison oak that thrives among these bushes. People who are immune to only mildly affected should have no problem if they take the usual precautions but hikers who are moderately to extremely sensitive should skip this trip. Carry water.

Drive on I-84 to the Multnomah Falls Exit 31. (You can also take the Scenic Highway to the falls.)

Take the pedestrian tunnel under the railroad tracks, cross the Scenic Highway and follow the wide, paved trail up to the bridge in front of the falls. Traverse out of the canyon and then travel along the north facing slope for about 0.1 mile to the first switchback and the junction of the Ak-Wanee Trail. (Refer to No. 17 for a description of the route to the right.)

Keep straight (east) on the unpaved tread and continue traversing. At 0.6 mile come to the edge of a large scree slope and just before its east end be on the lookout for a faint tread and the remnants of an old link fence. These are about 20 feet before the main trail rounds a corner. (See No. 18 for details of the route east.)

Turn uphill and follow the old tread. You'll have a bit of a tangle getting past the fence but beyond it the going is relatively easy, at least for a while. Although it's futile at the most overgrown of the switchbacks, try to stay on the trail as much as possible. If the alignment is destroyed by excessive shortcutting, a part of history and much of the fun and the scenic attraction of the route will be forever lost.

After about eight switchbacks come to a band of vegetation. Thrash through it, attempting to stay generally on the same alignment you had been following — don't veer to the west side of the scree. Beyond the bank of plants the going is again reasonably well defined until a hundred or so linear feet below the crest. Angle slightly right and follow the course of least resistance up to the saddle.

Turn right and walk gradually downhill along an obvious path. Pass a spiney, grass covered ridge a short distance before coming to the exposed viewpoint where you'll be able to peer down onto the parking lot for Multnomah Falls, a portion of the trail and into the canyon holding Multnomah Creek.

Knowledgeable hikers are encouraged to try the loop. From the saddle at 1.5 miles head southeast along the crest. Soon begin climbing, still on a trail, and after gaining about 400 feet of elevation come to the northwest edge of Multnomah Basin where the tread stops. The next 0.3 mile is the tricky part: You don't want to be right near the Gorge rim but neither do you want to veer too far right or you'll never intercept a road, which runs in generally a northeast-southwest direction. So, head pretty much in the same direction (east) as you were when you met the basin. Where you reach the road turn right and farther on where a spur heads right keep left. In the past, small red tags have pointed the way to Multnomah Falls. Meet a larger road, turn right, eventually cross a bridge and about 100 yards farther be watching for a path heading sharply off to your right that meets the highwater route of Multnomah Creek Trail No. 441.

Multnomah Falls Lodge parking lot from viewpoint

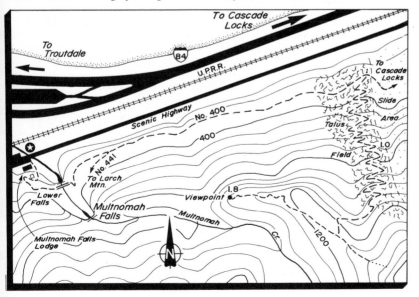

23 NESMITH RIDGE LOOP

One day trip
Distance: 5.9 miles round trip
Elevation gain: 2,500 feet
High point: 2,550 feet
Allow 4 to 5 hours round trip
Usually open mid March through mid
    December
Topographic maps:
  U.S.G.S. Bridal Veil, Wash.-Oreg.
  7.5'   1954
  U.S.G.S. Tanner Butte, Wash.-Oreg.
  7.5'   1979

Occasionally, the alignment of an abandoned route is such that it's not obliterated by windfall or ground cover and one of these old treads is the connector between the Nesmith Point Trail and the end of the route to Upper Elowah Falls on McCord Creek. The first half and the final mile of the loop are among the most scenic in the Gorge and with 2,500 feet of climbing in those initial three miles, the hike also provides a good workout. Although the abandoned connector has no exposure (or poison oak) and is reasonably easy going, the loop is *only* for experienced hikers with good route finding instincts. Those attempting the loop need enough savvy to recognize if they're hopelessly off course and that they need to retrace the route. For your first time it's recommended you make the loop prior to mid May before the foliage has fully leafed because be-

ing able to see ahead to Upper Elowah Falls from the 4.7 mile point is beneficial, both pyschologically and for route finding purposes. Begin with adequate water in case sources before McCord Creek aren't flowing.

Drive east of Portland on I-84 to the Ainsworth Park Exit 35. At the end of the exit turn left and after 150 feet turn right onto the frontage road. Head east, paralleling the freeway, 2.2 miles to a large parking area on your right at Yeon State Park.

Follow the trail from the west side of the parking area, switch back and in 75 feet come to the junction of the Gorge Trail No. 400 (see No. 19). Turn right and meander up through woods for 1.0 mile to a bridge. Turn left — don't cross the span — and traverse uphill. Cross over the rim into a basin and cross from side to side as you wind up. Enter a second, higher basin and again cross from side to side, entirely leaving it once. Where you come to the narrow crest at the top of the upper basin the main trail turns sharply right (see No. 24).

To make the loop, turn left at the crest. The lay of the land, blazes burned on trees and/or sections of tread make the route finding reasonably easy. After a few series of short ups and downs along the crest or just below it (*always* on the east — right — side), switch back and head straight down. Have a longer traverse on a rubble and debris strewn slope and then return to the crest where the footing is much better. Continue along the crest and climb from a little saddle. Coming up is a crucial route finding point: At the top of that short rise look left of an uprooted trunk for a blaze to the left and descend to it. You'll now be on the more westerly of two ridges. (If you'd missed that blaze and had continued in the same direction you had been heading, you'd be on the more easterly — and wrong — one.) Farther on, twice descend off to the right to avoid rock outcroppings, traverse and then rejoin the crest.

Beyond the final return to the crest the descent becomes more gentle and the vegetation lusher. Continue in the same direction, trying to follow blazes but definitely not veering left. If the foliage isn't fully out, you should be able to glimpse Upper Elowah Falls — aim for it. Come to a level strip that looks like an overgrown old road. Find a big blaze and a faint red arrow somewhat obscurely painted on a tree just beyond the opposite side of the road. A path angles down to the right (east) here. Locating the start of this tread is the second (and last) crucial route finding problem because trying to head cross-country straight down to the main trail would be very rough going.

Turn left where you meet the main trail at McCord Creek, pass views of the falls and walk along a massive cliff face. Wind down to the trail to the lower falls and turn left.

Upper Elowah Falls

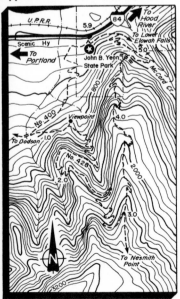

24 MOFFETT CREEK LOOP

One day trip
Distance: 11.5 miles round trip (14 miles round trip if Tanner Road gate is closed)
Elevation gain: 2,800 feet; loss 4,200 feet round trip
High point: 3,620 feet (3,880 feet at Nesmith Point)
Allow 6 to 7½ hours round trip (1 hour additional if gate is closed)
Usually open June through November
Topographic maps:
  U.S.G.S. Bridal Veil, Wash.-Oreg.
  15'   1954
  U.S.G.S. Tanner Butte, Oreg.-Wash.
  7.5'   1979

When the Moffett Creek Trail between Tanner Creek and Nesmith Point was reopened in 1980, hikers could explore this unfamiliar region with its several meadows and views of Mt. Talapus, neither common features in the Gorge. The recommended itinerary is to establish a car shuttle and return along the Nesmith Point Trail. Because of the ford of Tanner Creek, the trip is best done late in summer through early fall. Even at those times, though, pack tennis shoes for the crossing.

Drive on I-84 to the Ainsworth Park Exit 35. At the end of the exit turn left and 150 feet farther turn right onto the frontage road — don't rejoin the freeway. Travel east 2.2 miles to a large parking area on your right and leave one car here. Continue east to I-84 and take it 2.6 miles to the Bonneville Dam Exit 40. At the end of the exit turn right and then

several yards farther turn left onto graveled Road 777. After 0.2 mile curve sharply right, still on 777. In 1.1 miles keep straight where a spur branches off to the right (see No. 20), 1.1 miles farther pass the signed beginning of the Tanner Butte Trail and after another 0.6 mile come to a gate and park off the road here if the gate is closed.

Walk (or drive) along the road through woods and past several viewpoints for 2.5 miles to the signed beginning on your left of the Tanner Cutoff and Tanner Creek Trails. If the road has been reopened to public travel, DO NOT drive beyond this point.

Meander through woods for 0.6 mile to the junction of Trail No. 448, stay straight (right) and traverse, crossing many small side streams. At about 1.4 miles pass an unsigned spur to a campsite and 0.1 mile farther come to the marked junction of the Moffett Creek Trail. The Tanner Creek Trail continues another 0.5 mile before petering out.

Turn right, descend to the ford of Tanner Creek and begin winding steeply uphill for a short distance. As you climb at a more moderate grade in two dozen switchbacks past continually changing combinations of vegetation you'll have views of Mt. Talapus in the Bull Run Reserve, Mt. Hood and Tanner Butte. At 3.4 miles come to Von Ahn Rim, follow along it and then resume climbing.

Keep right at an unsigned fork and soon pass a large meadow with a tarn. Walk through another section of more open terrain, descend briefly to a power line access road and cross it. A short distance farther cross Moffett Creek and then the cleared swath under the lines, veering slightly right to pick up the signed trail. Begin descending, cross a fork of McCord Creek and after a wee climb have a longer downhill stretch. Glimpse a meadow off to your left just before crossing good-sized McCord Creek. Climb at an erratic grade, keep straight (left) at an unsigned fork and continue up to a road.

Turn right, descend and then a few hundred feet after you begin climbing pass the upper end of the Horsetail Creek Trail No. 425. Continue up the road and about 100 feet beyond a switchback to the right come to the signed Nesmith Point Trail on your right. To make the side trip to Nesmith Point, continue up the road for 0.5 mile.

To complete the hike, descend along the Nesmith Point Trail, curve left and begin a 1.6 mile traverse. Turn sharply left at the top of a narrow ridge (see No. 23) and wind down through terrain that is among the most scenic in the Gorge. Twice leave the huge basins on the left (west) sides and after the second time traverse to a bridge. Turn right onto the Gorge Trail (see No. 19) — don't cross the bridge — descend to the junction of the trail to Elowah Falls, turn left and walk the 150 feet to where you left the first car.

Munra Point from Tanner Creek Road

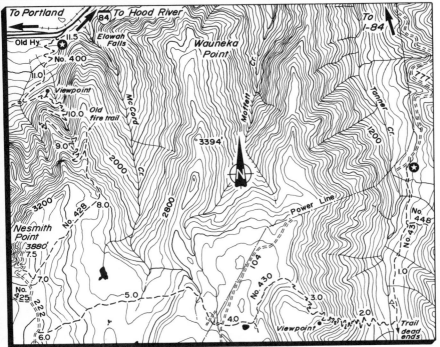

RUDOLPH SPUR LOOP

One day trip
Distance: 10.2 miles round trip
Elevation gain: 3,900 feet
High point: 3,740 feet
Allow 6 hours round trip
Usually open June through November
Topographic maps:
  U.S.G.S. Bonneville Dam, Wash.-Oreg.
  7.5′   1979
  U.S.G.S. Carson, Wash.-Oreg.
  7.5′   1979

The circuit up the Rudolph Spur Trail and down the Ruckel Creek Trail is an outing aficionados of strenuous Gorge loops will love. It's a bit harder than the classic Ruckel Ridge-Ruckel Creek loop but not as demanding as the Starvation Ridge-Mt. Defiance circuit. Some sections of the Rudolph Spur Trail are rustic (and steep), which is probably just fine with super-looper types who also tend to enjoy a change from manicured treads. In addition to being a fun challenge, the trip offers exceptional scenery and during mid to late April the hanging meadows midway along the descent support glorious wildflower displays. Present all through the hiking season are the panoramas up and down the Columbia River and the views north to Mt. Adams and south to Mt. Hood, as well as an 0.8 mile walk along an especially charming section of the Old Columbia River Highway. Begin with adequate water.

Drive on I-84 to the Cascade Locks Exit 44, follow the approach to the Bridge of the Gods and leave your car in the little park enclosed by the curve of the road.

From the exit of the park walk across the bridge approach road. Follow a trail for 100 yards, go under I-84 and meet a road. Turn right, in 75 feet keep straight on a dirt road and follow it 100 feet to the resumption of the PCT on your left. You'll be ending the loop across the road here. Initially head south along the PCT and then farther on curve east. At about 0.9 mile come to a narrow dirt road, turn right and follow it about 75 feet to the resumption of the trail on your left. Salamanders are abundant along this stretch so be careful not to step on any. Where you come to Dry Creek Road at 1.8 miles turn around and retrace your steps about 20 feet to a faint path heading south. (For a description of the Gorge Trail No. 400 that continues across the road, refer to No. 21.)

The tread of the Rudolph Spur Trail becomes more obvious after several yards and meanders uphill, occasionally along more open terrain. You can thank John Carlson of Cascade Locks for reopening this old route. Beyond the traverse of a large scree slope at 2.6 miles the tread is faint for a couple hundred feet as it climbs directly up a very steep slope. Beyond that pitch the route is obvious but the grade is only a bit less severe. Pass a little open ridge and farther on at 3.5 miles come to a considerably larger open area of little ground cover where you'll have the first far-ranging views. Walk up a natural corridor here to a bigger clearing and veer left along its lower edge to a sign stating Ruckel Creek Trail 1½. Not only is the steep uphill over here but you'll be on a high grade trail, at least until the final 0.5 mile before the junction with the Ruckel Creek Trail. However, yellow dobs of paint on tree trunks make this obscure alignment easy to follow.

At the junction with the Ruckel Creek Trail turn right and begin a moderately steep descent. A good place for a snack stop is near the small stream in the highest hanging meadow at 6.0 miles. Traverse through more meadows and then resume winding down in woods. Soon pass a dramatic viewpoint on the rim of the Gorge and after several more switchbacks travel through an immense rocky basin. Continue down to the Old Columbia River Highway and the junction of the Gorge Trail No. 400. You'll have a good water source where the trail passes near Ruckel Creek just before the road. Turn right, walk along the road for 0.8 mile and then follow a trail to the beginning of the loop. (For a more detailed description of the Gorge Trail that heads west and east from the 8.1 mile point refer to No. 20.)

Viewpoint along the trail

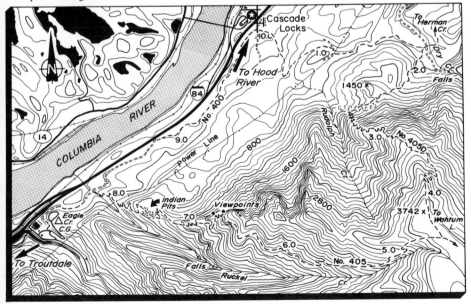

26 POWERLINE ACCESS TRAIL

One day trip
Distance: 3.7 miles as a loop
Elevation gain: 1,300 feet
High point: 1,100 feet
Allow 2½ hours for the loop
Usually open February through December
Topographic map:
  U.S.G.S. Mt. Defiance, Oreg.-Wash.
  7.5'   1979

Although some people avoid any trail that isn't relatively wide and smooth, most hikers enjoy occasionally exploring lower grade routes. A fun little trip for these latter types follows an abandoned section of the Old Columbia River Highway east from the Starvation Creek Rest Area and then climbs along rubbly old powerline access paths to viewpoints. Those who want a bit more of an adventure can continue west from the second viewpoint at 2.0 miles and do the trip as a loop. A good time to make this hike, particularly the loop, is the first half of April when the wildflowers are out but the bushes that line portions of the upper sections are not. Also, the poison oak that is along a few stretches is less robust then.

Proceed east on I-84 to the Starvation Creek Rest Area located 0.2 mile before the 55 mile post. After the hike you'll need to continue only 1.0 mile east along the freeway to the Viento Park Interchange. If you're approaching from the east, travel on I-84 to the Wyeth Interchange near mile post 51 and continue east on I-84 to the rest area.

Walk to the restroom building and continue east along the path from the south (men's) side several yards to a three-way fork. The route to the right goes to the base of Starvation Creek Falls, which definitely merits a visit. A bit of dramatic license was used in naming the stream because, although in 1884 two trains were stranded here during a blizzard, in fact aid and supplies came in time so no one actually starved.

Keep straight on the road and soon begin traveling along a portion of the old highway. After about 100 yards pass wooden stakes with numbers on your right. The path that heads up here is the one you'll be coming down if you make the loop. Continue along the road for another 0.7 mile to similar stakes stating 16-1/16-2 and 15-9/15-3. (These figures are the numbers of the powerline towers to which the trail goes.) The path you'll be taking begins here. The road continues east for another few tenths mile to near the Viento Park Interchange.

From those stakes at 1.0 mile begin winding uphill. If you opt not to make the loop, descending this path will be less of a problem than you might anticipate, given the loose stones that comprise the tread. Six-tenths mile from the road come to a fork, turn left and continue up a bit farther to the most easterly of the viewpoints.

To reach the middle viewpoint at 2.0 miles, which is an ideal turnaround point for those not making the loop, retrace your route to the fork and follow the other branch up past tower 15-9 to tower 15-8. The tread along this westerly route is considerably smoother than the part from the road to the fork. As from the easterly viewpoint, you'll be able to see down onto highway, rail and barge traffic, up and down the Columbia River and across it to Dog and Wind Mountains. The rocky spire protruding from the Gorge wall downriver on the Oregon side is Indian Point. If you want a face wash and drinking water, continue west along the path for a couple hundred feet to a stream.

To complete the loop, follow the path to the stream and continue contouring. Eventually, travel just below a tower and 50 feet farther come above another tower and follow the path that angles down to it. Continue west for a short distance and then head downslope for about 15 feet over a thick bed of old leaves. Turn left, resume traversing on a path to the last viewpoint, which is somewhat exposed and can be slippery when wet. From it descend in switchbacks along a considerably better defined and less vegetated trail to the old highway.

Trail view of Columbia River and Wind Mountain

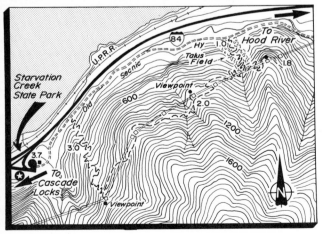

27 BEAR LAKE and MT. DEFIANCE

One day trip
Distance: 1.6 miles one way; 0.6 mile
additional one way to Bear Lake
Elevation gain: 1,110 feet; 200 feet
additional from Bear Lake
High point: 4,959 feet
Allow 1 hour one way
Usually open mid June through November
Topographic map:
U.S.G.S. Mt. Defiance, Oreg.-Wash.
7.5′   1979

Mt. Defiance is the highest point in the Columbia Gorge and, not surprisingly, the view from the summit is far ranging, including the major peaks from Mt. Rainier south to nearby Mt. Hood, a bird's eye view down over the Upper and Lower Hood River Valleys and beyond to the wheat fields of eastern Oregon. Climbing from I-84 to the summit of Mt. Defiance is a favorite conditioning trip for moun-

taineers but for hikers who don't feel like working that hard there's a considerably easier trail from the southwest. In addition to the side trip to Bear Lake, a very scenic 1.0 mile loop heads north and then south from the summit. Begin with adequate water.

Take I-84 to the West Hood River Exit 62. Turn right at its end, after 1.3 miles turn right onto 13th and continue following signs to Parkdale and Odell and then Dee through many turns for 11.8 miles to a road on your right that heads down to the lumber mill at Dee. (You also can reach Dee along Oregon 35 or from Lolo Pass (see No. 28).) Descend, cross the bridge and turn right, following the sign to Punch Bowl. Three-tenths mile beyond the bridge keep straight (right) and 1.1 miles farther stay straight again, now following the sign to Rainy Lake. The pavement ends just beyond here. The road bed is wash boardy so don't go too fast, particularly downhill. One-tenth mile beyond the end of the pavement stay left on 2820 to Rainy Lake and continue on 2820 at subsequent junctions. After 8.0 miles come to a T-junction, turn left, continuing on 2820, and travel the final 2.2 miles to a large sign on your right identifying the beginning of the Mt. Defiance and Wyeth Trails.

Walk 80 feet into the woods and turn right onto Trail No. 413. Climb gradually along the Mt. Defiance Trail for 0.5 mile to the junction of the 0.6 mile spur to shallow Bear Lake. If you're hiking later in the summer on a warm day, you might opt to visit the lake on the way back and enjoy a swim. This spur climbs gradually, crosses a small talus slope and then descends for the remaining distance to the lake.

To complete the hike to the summit, continue on the main trail and begin climbing more noticeably. Farther on switch back through a small swath of talus, just above it have a view down onto Bear Lake and continue up to a junction. If you make the highly recommended loop from the top, you'll be returning on the trail to the left. For now, keep right, wind up in three short switchbacks and head north for the final distance to the flat summit. A lookout tower once occupied the site of the present microwave installation.

To make the recommended loop, walk to the northeast corner of the building and look north for a large, old reddish-brown sign on a tree stating Mt. Defiance Trail. Follow the well defined path down to Road 2821, cross it and continue descending. Where you come to 2821 a second time veer right a few yards to pick up the tread. After about 0.2 mile more of downhill be watching for a trail heading off sharply on your left. It is signed but the marker is facing the other way. Turn left onto this trail and traverse for 0.6 mile to the trail you followed in, enjoying views not seen from the summit.

Bear Lake from Mount Defiance

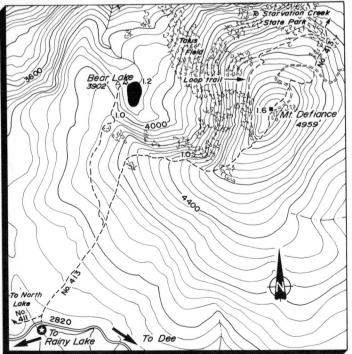

28 HICKS LAKE LOOP

One day trip
Distance: 6 miles round trip
Elevation gain: 1,000 feet
High point: 4,300 feet
Allow 3 hours round trip
Usually open late June through mid
    November
Topographic map:
  U.S.G.S. Wahtum Lake, Oreg.
  7.5'   1979

One of the easiest of the few reasonable cross country trips in the Gorge is the 0.8 mile segment from Hicks Lake to the Pacific Crest Trail. Hikers who aren't interested in following the 0.7 mile, long abandoned trail down to the lake or making the cross-country can enjoy just the easterly half of the figure eight loop, which circles Wahtum Lake and visits Chinidere Mountain with its views of Mounts St. Helens, Rainier, Adams and Hood, the Columbia River and many Gorge landmarks. Begin with adequate water.

You can make the first part of the drive either along US 26 or I-84. For the former head east of Portland about 42 miles to the community of Zigzag, turn north onto East Lolo Pass Road and after 10.9 miles come to the pass. Head down the other side on Road 18 (which is unpaved for 3.3 miles) 10.3 miles to its junction with Road 13. Turn right and 3.1 miles farther turn sharply left, staying on 13, which may not be identified as such, but has a stop sign. Follow 13, which has an oiled surface, for 4.5 miles to the junction of 1310. Keep right and

continue on paved 1310 for 6.2 miles to Wahtum Lake Campground.

Or, take I-84 to the West Hood River Exit 62. Turn right at its end, after 1.3 miles turn right onto 13th and continue following signs to Parkdale and Odell and then Dee through many turns for 11.8 miles to a road on your right that heads down to the lumber mill at Dee. Descend, cross the bridge and turn left. Follow Lost Lake Road, which eventually becomes 13, 5.0 miles to the junction of 13 on your right (at this point the two roads are numbered the same) and continue as described above.

From the campground walk downhill for 0.3 mile to Wahtum Lake and the junction of the PCT. Turn right, travel above the lake and then climb to the junction at 1.9 miles with the connector to the Herman Creek Trail. Turn left and after several hundred feet come to the junction of Trail No. 445, which you'll be taking on the way back. Stay straight on the PCT and in 175 feet pass the 0.2 mile spur up to Chinidere Mountain. Contour across an open slope that around early July supports an astounding variety of wildflowers. Enter woods and begin traversing downhill. Come to a saddle and beyond it begin traveling gradually uphill, with a couple of level stretches. About 1.0 mile beyond the junction of the Chinidere Mountain spur descend again for a short distance and then resume climbing to an open area and the unsigned, obscure junction on your right of the Hicks Lake Trail. A short snag here just below the PCT on the left has a block of wood nailed to its south facing side and the slope on the right is an exposed, steep bank of dirt.

Scramble up the bank for several feet, veer right and follow the overgrown tread. Traverse up to the southeast, soon leaving the dense vegetation, make two short switchbacks and come to a crest. Walk southeast along it and then begin descending. After 0.7 mile of the downhill traverse you'll be able to see Hicks Lake and a short distance farther the tread disappears in a tangle of blowdown. Head cross country down to a camp area in the woods near the south shore. A small spring is several yards west of the fire pit.

Head cross country to the southeast up from the lake for about 0.4 mile to a saddle. Once you're above the tangle of blowdown near the lake the going, though steep, is relatively easy. At the crest veer right and travel gradually down through open woods until you intersect the connector to the Herman Creek Trail. Turn right, meet the PCT and continue to the junction of Trail No. 445. Turn left onto No. 445, descend and then climb from the outlet of Wahtum Lake to the Eagle Creek Trail. Turn left, walk along the south shore, keep straight (left) at the junction of the PCT and continue east to the trail you took down from the campground.

Mounts Rainier and Adams from Chinidere Mountain

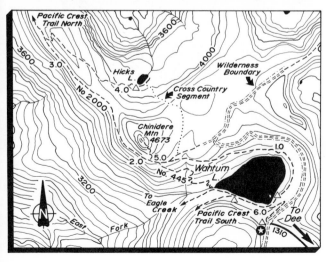

northern oregon cascades

When visitors recall a region like the High Sierra of California usually one quintessential image comes to mind. But when people think of the northern Oregon Cascades many mental pictures jostle for prominence: Mounts Hood and Jefferson with their girdles of exquisite timberline scenes; woods of robust Douglas fir, elegant cedars, moss draped lodgepole pines and nurse logs supporting little cities of seedlings; rambunctious streams and rivers; highpoints with panoramas of both wilderness and the works of man; slopes of wildflowers; patches of huckleberry bushes; and the many miles of trails that wend amoung these multifarious scenes. The 22 hikes in this section sample all these aspects of the northern Oregon Cascades plus a few that might not come to mind so readily, such as excellent alpine swimming lakes.

One of the biggest recent changes in the Oregon outdoors was the creation in June, 1984, of 23 new Wildernesses and additions to seven existing ones. In the northern Oregon Cascades these new preserves include the Columbia in the Eagle and Herman Creek drainages of the Columbia Gorge (No. 28), Badger Creek southeast of Mt. Hood, Salmon-Huckleberry (No's. 32, 33, 39 and 40) southwest of Mt. Hood, Bull of the Woods (No's. 47, 48 and 49) between Mounts Hood and Jefferson and Table Rock (No. 46) southeast of Molalla.

With the exception of Hiyu Mountain (No. 31), which is short but not commenserately easy, and the Green Canyon-Salmon River (No. 33) and Lamberson Spur (No. 36) Loops, which are very long and very hard, the trips in this section are moderate in length and elevation gain. All can be done as one day hikes although 16 of the 22 do connect with other routes. So, you can make longer outings, if you wish. Three (No's. 34, 47 and 48) make excellent backpacks because they end at locations which make perfect base camps from which to explore other trails and landmarks. If you plan to travel beyond the descriptions given here or make any of those backpacks, you should purchase a recreation map (cost $1) for the Mt. Hood National Forest. One is available from the US Forest Service Information Office at 319 SW Pine in Portland, headquarters for the Mt. Hood National Forest in Gresham or any of the ranger stations. You also can refer to *62 Hiking Trails — Northern Oregon Cascades* by Don and Roberta Lowe. One of those recreation maps is indispensable when you want to identify landmarks comprising the panoramas seen from the summits of Table Rock (No. 46), Whetstone Mountain (No. 47) and Bull of the Woods (No. 49).

For the hikes in this section carry all the essentials in your pack — wool hat, gloves, sweater, windbreaker, waterproof garmet, first aid kit, map of the area, compass (assuming you know how to use it), flashlight and a little extra food. Also include sun screen and mosquito repellent. An effective combination of the latter is a lotion for skin and a spray for clothing. Fords shouldn't be necessary for any of the hikes in this section because the big streams are bridged. If you ever do have to make a ford one of the best of several alternatives is to take off your socks, wear your boots across and then put the dry socks back on. If you know ahead you'll be making a ford, carry along a pair of tennis shoes for the crossing. Never ford barefoot because you'll likely cut or bruise your feet. Don't ever hesitate to turn back if you come to a ford, or any terrain, that you don't feel is safe. While on the subject of water, most likely you wouldn't be obtaining drinking water from a stream that is glacier fed because it looks so unappetizing. As the glacier moves it grinds up rocks and the resulting fine particles give the streams their milky appearance. Aside from not looking nor tasting good, this grit irritates the G.-I. tract. Water from snow fed streams is fine, assuming there are no pollutants.

Fortunately, the northern Oregon Cascades aren't like the Colorado Rockies where the sky can go from cloudless to a raging thunderstorm in an hour. But lightning does occur here and if you note a storm building get off summits and ridge tops and head for deep timber — not a lone tree.

On lands managed by the US Forest Service trail maintenance schedules vary but each year the most heavily used routes are cleared of blowdown, slides, etc. Primarily because of limited funds, secondary trails are maintained less frequently and often not to as high a standard. However, in Wildernesses there's a definite policy, regardless of available moneys, to have lower standards because part of the reason for these areas is the preservation of a reasonably natural, not a manicured, ambience for visitors.

29 RED HILL

One day trip
Distance: 2.2 miles one way
Elevation gain: 550 feet; loss 200 feet
High point: 4,950 feet
Allow 1 hour one way
Usually open late June through October
Topographic map:
  U.S.G.S. Cathedral Ridge, Oreg.
  7.5′   1962

From most angles, Red Hill is an undistinguished bump on the northwestern flank of Mt. Hood. But from the right perspective, the swath of brick colored volcanic rock that caps the north end of Blue Ridge makes Red Hill a unique and unmistakable landmark. The view from it to other features is equally noteworthy and includes an excellent — and photogenic — view of Mt. Hood. With the red cinders in the foreground and the chance of alpenglow on the peak, this is an especially good hike for late in the afternoon. Just be sure to pack a flashlight if there's a chance you'll be coming out in the dark. The route to Red Hill follows the Vista Ridge Trail for the initial 0.4 mile so hikers who want a longer day could take it up for 2.2 miles more to the junction with the Timberline Trail at Wy'east Basin (see No. 34) and then continue even farther through the exquisite alpine setting. Note that the final 0.2 mile to Red Hill is cross country. Carry water.

Drive east of Portland on US 26 about 42 miles to the community of Zigzag and turn north onto East Lolo Pass Road, which eventually becomes 18. After 10.9 miles come to Lolo Pass where the pavement temporarily ends. (Hikes No's. 30 and 31 begin here.) Head downhill at a junction 3.3 miles below the pass, keep straight (left) on 18 and resume traveling on a paved surface. After another 3.3 miles turn sharply right onto paved Road 16, as indicated by the sign pointing to Vista Ridge Trail. Stay on 16 for 5.4 miles to the junction of Road 1650. Turn right onto the unpaved surface and stay on 1650 for 3.6 miles to its end at the signed trailhead. The final 0.4 mile is very rough but is level and passable.

From the sign walk along an open, rubbly and overgrown area, obviously the uncompleted extension of the road. Beyond the abandoned construction enter woods and climb gently along a smooth trail to a T-junction. The main route No. 626 heads right to the Timberline Trail.

To reach Red Hill, turn left and continue gradually uphill. Switch back and farther on come to a less heavily wooded saddle. Continue through the more open terrain of an old burn and then resume traversing an east facing slope, occasionally traveling past large rock outcroppings. At about 1.6 miles come to a mostly treeless crest and then descend to a little meadow.

Follow the trail for about 100 feet into the meadow, turn left and follow a wide treeless band that soon becomes a swale. About 300 feet from the big meadow come to a smaller one where the swale curves left. Veer right here and begin climbing. Note landmarks because it's recommended that you follow the same route back. The course of least resistance is to bear slightly right. After about 200 yards from where you left the swale come to the open area just below the ridge crest, turn left (west) and go the final few hundred feet to the summit. Walk along the upper edge of the red rocks, which you'll meet just before the top, because any footprints in the lava will remain a long time and their presence lessens the naturalness of the scene.

Sightings include unobstructed views of what you periodically glimpsed along the hike in, such as the buildings at Cloud Cap. Yocum Ridge forms the right skyline on Mt. Hood and Cooper Spur the left with Cathedral Ridge the one in between. The flat-topped peak with the lookout to the southwest is Hickman Butte in the Bull Run Reserve.

Mount Hood from Red Hill

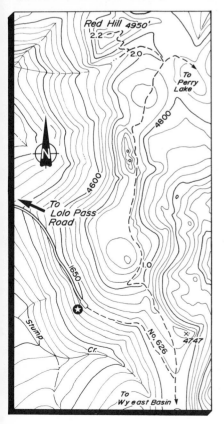

30 LOLO PASS to BALD MOUNTAIN

One day trip
Distance: 3.3 miles one way
Elevation gain: 1,400 feet; loss 200 feet
High point: 4,591 feet
Allow 2 hours one way
Usually open late June through October
Topographic maps:
U.S.G.S. Bull Run Lake, Oreg.
7.5′   1962
U.S.G.S. Cathedral Ridge, Oreg.
7.5′   1962

The 3.1 mile section of the Pacific Crest Trail from Lolo Pass to the junction with the Timberline Trail on the northwest flank of Bald Mountain isn't heavily used because there's a considerably shorter route to the same intersection from Road 118. Not hiking those extra miles makes sense for people heading to Cairn Basin or other destinations farther along the Timberline or Pacific Crest Trails but the section from Lolo Pass definitely is worth a hike in itself. The woods are consistently lush yet surprisingly varied in character and one viewpoint offers an uncommon view to the northeast that includes Mt. Adams and several landmarks in the Columbia Gorge. A 0.3 mile spur heads up from the junction of the PCT and Timberline Trail to the summit of Bald Mountain and a face-to-face look at Mt. Hood. Begin with adequate water.

Proceed east of Portland on US 26 about 42 miles to the community of Zigzag, turn left onto East Lolo Pass Road and follow it 10.9 miles to Lolo Pass

where signs mark sections of the PCT heading north and south. (Hike No. 31 also begins from the pass.)

Head south along the PCT, following the sign pointing to Timberline Trail, through a clearcut and then enter woods. Since rhododendrons are thick here the hike would be especially attractive around late June when they're blooming. Make 10 switchbacks and then near 1.6 miles travel just above a bushy bench with a little pond. Have a long traverse and farther on walk along the crest of the ridge. That view of the valley holding the West Fork of the Hood River, highpoints in the Gorge such as Indian Mountain, Chinidere Mountain (No. 28) and Mt. Defiance (No. 27) and Mt. Adams is more obvious on the way back, so don't fret if you miss it on the hike in.

Walk gently downhill and have glimpses of Mt. Hood behind the trees, keep straight (left) where the unsigned 0.5 mile connector comes up from Road 118 and a couple hundred feet farther meet a four-way junction. The trail to the left is the portion of the Timberline Trail that heads to McNeil Point, Cairn Basin and other points north and east. The far right section was the former alignment of the Timberline-Pacific Crest Trails and it joins the north end of the Ramona Falls Loop. The middle route is the newer, current alignment of the PCT-Timberline Trail and meets the Ramona Falls Loop just west of Ramona Falls.

A shelter, one of the nine that once stood along or near the Timberline Trail, used to occupy what is now the clearing on the northeast corner of the intersection. All that remain today are the stone huts at Paradise Park, McNeil Point and Cairn Basin and the wooden, three-sided shelter at Elk Meadows. Stone buildings once were also at Elk Cove, Cooper Spur and Gnarl Ridge and wooden ones at Ramona Falls and here near Bald Mountain. Avalanches did in the stone buildings and vandals the wooden ones.

Take the middle route and 100 feet beyond the Wilderness bulletin board look for an unsigned trail on your left. Take it, parallel the main route for a few yards and then climb to the summit. Keep walking for several yards until you're on the open east face and have an unobstructed view of Mt. Hood.

A section of the PCT-Timberline Trail is obvious directly below and if you look across and up the valley holding the Muddy Fork you can spot another section traversing along the north wall of Yocum Ridge. That portion up from the river was (and continues to be) a problem for work crews as the slope is prone to slippage. People who want a bit more hiking could follow the PCT-Timberline Trail along the rocky south side of Bald Mountain until the route re-enters the woods. In addition to providing more views, this open slope supports many wildflowers.

Mount Hood from summit of Bald Mountain

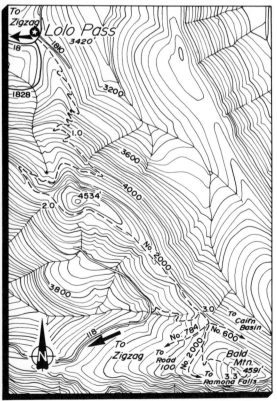

31 HIYU MOUNTAIN

One day trip
Distance: 1.3 miles one way
Elevation gain: 1,220 feet
High point: 4,654 feet
Allow ¾ hour one way
Usually open June through October
Topographic map:
U.S.G.S. Bull Run Lake, Oreg.
7.5′   1962

Hiyu Mountain is directly above and northwest of Lolo Pass. Although the panorama from the summit extends from Mounts St. Helens, Rainier and Adams in Washington south past Olallie Butte to Mt. Jefferson in Oregon, the most eye-catching landmark is the west face of Mt. Hood just four air miles away. The price hikers pay for the short distance to such a superb viewpoint is a few hundred feet of messy cross-country climbing near the start of the trip. Once found, though, the abandoned trail is easy to follow. If you want more hiking you can continue north along the Pacific Crest Trail toward Buck Peak or southeast to Bald Mountain (No. 30). Carry water.

Drive on US 26 for 42 miles east of Portland to the community of Zigzag and turn north onto East Lolo Pass Road. Follow the road, which eventually becomes Road 18, 10.9 miles to Lolo Pass and park at the sign identifying the section of the PCT that heads north.

Follow the PCT for 0.2 mile to a cat road heading left under the topmost powerline and turn onto it. These open slopes under the lines are dense with rhododendron bushes which are a mass of pink when they're blooming in late June. After walking along the cat road for several yards turn right and scramble uphill. After several more yards come to a narrow, overgrown road, turn right, follow it a hundred feet or so and then head upslope into the timber, bearing slightly left and following the course of least resistance. About 75 linear feet above the upper edge of the powerline cut you should meet the trail. New blowdown seems to be methodically obliterating the eastern-most portion of the tread — not too many years ago you could begin the hike from the east side of the slope. If you have trouble locating the route, go a bit farther west. However, don't go too far because the trail angles up to the northwest. Confront another tangle of blowdown soon after the route curves upslope and then begin traveling along a relatively clean trail, considering how long it's been abandoned.

As you're encouraged to do on all hikes, flick away twigs, rocks and other debris. Doing so for trails that are maintained enables crews to spend their time on bigger projects and for routes like this one your efforts will contribute to keeping them passable. Meet a set of switchbacks and, farther on, another pair. Unless new blowdown has blocked the tread, make every effort to stay on the trail — don't fuzzy-up the alignment by shortcutting. From the final switchback walk up a crest, travel on the northeast side of the ridge then cross to the southwest side and plow through a brushy stretch to a road. Note these final several yards for the return trip. Turn right, climb a few yards to the former lookout site and for the best views continue east to the end of the ridge.

You'll have a fine perspective of all the main features on the west face of Mt. Hood from Vista Ridge on the left skyline past Barrett Spur, Cathedral and Yocum Ridges and Bald Mountain to the cliffs just above Paradise Park on the right skyline. Red Hill (No. 29) is in the middle distance north of Mt. Hood, a bit of the Lower Hood River Valley is visible and features in the Columbia Gorge such as Mt. Defiance (No. 27) and Indian Mountain are to the north. As you walk back from the lookout site you can see down onto Bull Run Lake in the Bull Run Reserve, which begins on the north side of the road and is absolutely closed to public entry.

Bull Run Lake from Hiyu Mountain

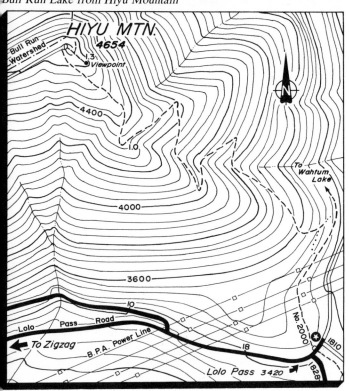

32 BOULDER RIDGE

One day trip
Distance: 5.4 miles one way
Elevation gain: 3,400 feet
High point: 4,350 feet
Allow 3 hours one way
Usually open late May through
**   mid November**
Topographic maps:
** U.S.G.S. Cherryville, Oreg.**
** 15'   1955**
** U.S.G.S. Rhododendron, Oreg.**
** 7.5'   1962**

The Boulder Ridge Trail, completed in the spring of 1981, winds up through the northwestern corner of the even newer (1984) Salmon-Huckleberry Wilderness past several overlooks. It ends at a viewpoint that affords, in addition to sightings of the major peaks from Mounts Rainier to Jefferson, uncommon perspectives of the Columbia River and landmarks in the Columbia Gorge.

Drive on US 26 about 40 miles from Portland or 2.4 miles west of Zigzag to a sign on the south side of the highway marking the entrance to the Wildwood Recreation Site. (If you're doing the hike early or late in the season and the entrance is closed be sure not to block the gate when you park.) Drive (or walk) south along the access road for 0.2 mile, keep straight (left) per the sign pointing to trailhead, and continue 0.3 mile farther to a large parking area.

The trail begins from the north side of the restrooms and crosses an elegant bridge over the Salmon River. Walk on the level through an attractive alder grove and cross a little bridge. Just beyond it keep left and begin climbing, alternating among switchbacks, traverses and meanderings. At one turn farther on have a view of Mt. Hood and Hunchback Ridge (see No. 33). If you make the hike the first part of July you'll be a couple of weeks late for the prime rhododendron and beargrass displays, but just right for the blooms of columbine, foxglove, wild iris, daisy and, at the destination, phlox.

At 1.8 miles come to an old logging road, which with each passing year looks more like a trail. Turn left onto the bed and traverse for 0.3 mile to the end of the road where the ground cover abruptly ceases and the woods consist entirely of old growth conifers. Continue traversing, hop a small stream and then switchback twice. Cross over the nose of a ridge and begin a long traverse on the east facing slope to a saddle. Along this stretch the character of the woods again changes — rhododendrons and its frequent neighbor beargrass provide ground cover and the trees, though smaller, are draped with moss.

As you traverse beyond the saddle along a west facing slope you'll be able to see ahead to Huckleberry Mountain ridge, to Wildcat Mountain and between those two highpoints down into Boulder Creek valley, probably about the least visited region in the Mt. Hood area. Come to another saddle, farther on cross a stream, the last source of water, and climb to the junction of the old Plaza Trail at a crest at 4.2 miles. The overgrown route down to the north, though exceptionally interesting, was abandoned because it ends on private property.

Turn right, climb, descend and then climb past foot tripping beargrass to open slopes. As you travel the final distance you'll have views northwest over the Columbia River and at the destination you can leisurely identify Devils Peak (see No. 33) and Salmon Mountain (No. 40), north past West Zigzag Mountain, Hickman Butte (the flat topped one with the lookout) and Lolo Pass to highpoints in the Columbia Gorge such as Tanner Butte, Chinidere Mountain (see No. 28) and Indian Mountain and Mt. St. Helens in Washington. You were promised a view of Mt. Jefferson but you'll have to look south beyond the tree tops for just its tip. The main trail continues over the summit of Huckleberry Mountain to a junction where one route heads northwest to Wildcat Mountain and another southeast down to the Salmon River along the Bonanza Trail.

Wild Iris

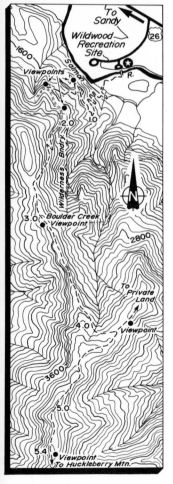

33 GREEN CANYON — SALMON RIVER LOOP

One day trip
Distance: 13.3 miles round trip
Elevation gain: 4,000 feet
High point: 5,045 feet
Allow 8 to 9 hours round trip
Usually open late June through October
Topographic maps:
  U.S.G.S. Government Camp, Oreg.
  7.5'   1962
  U.S.G.S. High Rock, Oreg.
  15'   1956
  U.S.G.S. Rhododendron, Oreg.
  7.5'   1962

The newest trail in the Mt. Hood National Forest is the tread that begins near Green Canyon Campground on the Salmon River and climbs for 2.6 miles to the crest of Hunchback Ridge where it meets the long established route there. The Green Canyon Trail was only half completed by the fall of 1985 and, because of lack of funds, may not even be finished in 1986. However, the upper portion of the eventual alignment is not difficult to follow and hikers who don't mind a modest challenge will enjoy seeing what a partially completed trail is like. Be sure to allow plenty of time because this demanding loop is exceptionally scenic and you don't want to be so tired or rushed that you can't savor the views from Devils Peak or the final stretch along the Salmon River.

Drive on US 26 for 42 miles east of Portland to the Salmon River Road just before the community of Zigzag, turn right (south) and proceed 5.1 miles to the parking turnouts on either side of the road just before the bridge at the beginning of the Upper Salmon River Trail, along which you'll be returning.

Walk back (north) along the Salmon River Road about 200 yards to a weathered little wooden sign on a tree on your left where the Lower Salmon River Trail briefly meets the road. Look directly across the road from this sign for a path heading into the woods. After a hundred feet or so this path becomes a proper trail. After three irregularly spaced switchbacks cross over the nose of a ridge, soon come to a fork on an open slope and turn left. Continue up in woods and eventually come to a very short stretch of rock. Even if it hasn't been blasted out yet, it's no problem to traverse. Resume traveling along a good tread for two switchbacks to where the work ended as of 1985. Assuming further construction hasn't been done, continue in the same direction from the end of the tread for a couple of hundred feet but be watching upslope for cut logs. This section coming up and an even shorter one farther on are the only stretches of steepish, rough terrain. Make the faint switchback, traverse past the cuts, switch back and resume traveling on an obvious tread to a crest.

Turn right at the crest to reach a viewpoint and left to continue the hike. Travel up the crest for a short distance and then veer off to the left, following blazes. After a few hundred yards head up to the crest on your right and follow along it. Be watching downslope on your left for signs of cut logs and when you see them drop off the crest. Your route finding challenges are over because the remaining 0.6 mile to Trail No. 793 is either along a tread or an alignment marked by cut logs.

At the junction of the trail that travels along Hunchback Ridge from Zigzag to Devils Peak turn right and head along the crest, mostly at a gentle uphill grade but with a few steep pulls. Pass through two delightful meadows straddling the ridgetop. The path at 4.9 miles down to the first water source is identified by a sign. At the junction of the spur to Devils Peak stay right to reach the lookout where the view extends from Mt. Rainier to Three Fingered Jack.

After the side trip, traverse along the north facing slope, stay right at the junction of the Cool Creek Trail and continue mostly downhill across open slopes and then in woods to the end of the Sherar Burn Road. Walk along it for 150 feet to the Kinzel Lake Trail on your right. Follow it down past a jungle of rhododendrons and continue winding down to the Salmon River Trail. Turn right and follow the trail for the remaining 5.4 miles to the road.

Cedar and fir along the trial

34 PINNACLE RIDGE

One day trip or backpack
Distance: 4.3 miles one way to Elk Cove
Elevation gain: 2,100 feet; loss 300 feet to
Elk Cove
High point: 5,750 feet
Allow 2½ hours one way to Elk Cove
Usually open mid July through mid October
Topographic map:
U.S.G.S. Cathedral Ridge, Oreg.
15′ 1962

The Pinnacle Ridge Trail affords relatively short and easy access to the sublime timberline setting on the northwest side of Mt. Hood. Although the perky white blooms of avalanche lilies are common at higher elevations about the second week of July, they are especially profuse around the 3.0 mile point. As it would be on any hike, the trade-off for these enchanting displays is that you'll probably encounter some snow along the highest sections of the trail. From the junction of the Pinnacle Ridge Trail with the Timberline Trail at 3.3 miles hikers have the option of heading west for 0.1 mile to Wy'east Basin or 1.0 east down to Elk Cove. People with even more time and energy can climb Barrett Spur from Wy'east Basin. This is an ideal hike for establishing a base camp and making side trips from it.

Proceed on Oregon 35 for 16.5 miles from its junction with US 26 to the Cooper Spur Road, turn left and after 2.4 miles stay straight (right). In 5.3 miles turn left, following the signs pointing to Evans and Clear Creeks and Laurance Lake. Turn left again in 0.6 mile, continuing to follow signs to Laurance Lake and after 4.3 miles a short distance beyond where you come to the southeast end of Laurance Lake at Kinnikinnick Picnic Ground turn left, as indicated by the sign pointing to Elk Cove and Pinnacle Ridge. After 1.1 miles of unpaved, rough road keep straight (right), 1.9 miles farther (during which the road surface improves) turn left onto 670 and drive the final couple hundred feet to the signed trailhead.

Walk up through a cover of smallish conifers to a little clearing and beyond it enter deeper woods. Farther on skirt a scree slope and then come to a stream. Near 1.3 miles walk along the lower side of another rocky swath, have a short, steep, rooty section of trail and then continue up at a moderate grade to a sign marking the Wilderness boundary at a wee stream. Begin rising at a more persistent, though erratic, grade. Have a look left to The Pinnacle and then a glimpse ahead to Mt. Hood.

Near 2.5 miles come to a flat, marshy area that around mid July is a garden of avalanche lilies, elephant heads, heather, shooting stars and buttercups. At the meadow's south side resume climbing through increasingly alpine terrain. Where you come to an open swath and the tread is faint, continue up in the same direction for about 50 feet and then veer left onto an obvious tread and re-enter woods. Meet a swale, cross it and travel up the west (right) side. Come to a second, parallel ravine and again cross it and walk along its west side. Where the tread stops, climb in the same direction and in a short distance meet the Timberline Trail.

To visit Wy'east Basin, turn right. If it's late in the hiking season so the flow of Ladd Creek, which you ford twice, has moderated and you feel like another 2.5 miles of hiking you can make a loop by continuing west along the Timberline Trail from Wy'east Basin to Cairn Basin and following a former section of the Timberline Trail down through Eden Park to Trail No. 626 and taking it back up to Wy'east Basin.

To reach Elk Cove head east along the Timberline Trail from the junction at 3.3 miles. After 0.5 mile pass an unsigned path on your right that climbs an open slope for 0.3 mile to Dollar Lake. If you're camping at Elk Cove be sure to do so in the wooded areas, not the meadows. One of the original stone huts along the Timberline Trail used to be east of the stream. As the broken-off trees indicate, avalanches are common in the basin and they reduced the shelter to a low wall of stones. Forest Service people removed the remains.

Mt. Hood from the Timberline Trail

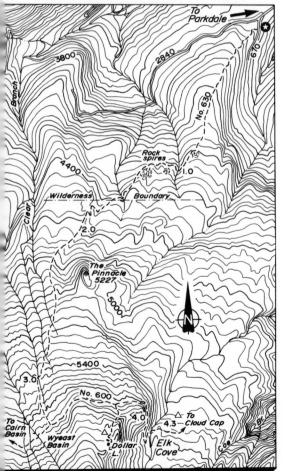

35 ELIOT GLACIER VIEW

One day trip
Distance: 2.5 miles one way
Elevation gain: 2,450 feet; loss 200 feet
High point: 8,050 feet
Allow 2 hours one way
Usually open late July through early October
Topographic map:
  U.S.G.S. Cathedral Ridge, Oreg.
  7.5'   1962

Usually, hikers need special skills and equipment for climbing high enough to come face-to-face with a glacier. One exception is the route on the north side of Mt. Hood to a viewpoint midway along Eliot Glacier, one of the most heavily crevassed on the peak. Wooded and flower splashed slopes along the lower portions of the trip provide a balance to the expanse of awesomely broken up ice and, as if the immediate scene weren't reward enough, the far ranging view extends over the Upper Hood River Valley and Columbia River to Mounts St. Helens, Rainier and Adams. The hike is best made in September when the snow along the route will be at a minimum. Be warned that one short section at 2.0 miles traverses a rocky face. Negotiating this traverse is not at all technically demanding but it is a contrast to the well used trail below and the easy cross country above. Begin with water.

Proceed on Oregon 35 for 16.5 miles east and north of its junction with US 26 to Cooper Spur Road. Turn left and in 2.4 miles turn left again, continuing to follow signs to the ski area. After 1.5 miles at its entrance keep right on unpaved Road 3512, 8.5 miles farther at the Tilly Jane junction keep right and travel the final 0.6 mile to turnouts on your right at a sign identifying the Timberline Trail No. 600.

Walk south through the camp area for a hundred feet or so to the Timberline Trail and turn right. Curve into the canyon holding Eliot Creek and cross it. After September the bridge most likely will have been removed for the year but the ford shouldn't be too difficult then. Wind up in seven short switchbacks and just beyond where you round the face of the ridge look left for an unsigned, but obvious, path heading up through a treeless patch.

Turn onto the path, follow it up to a little crest and then where you come to a hollow veer left and return to the crest. Very soon, and abruptly, come to the end of the dense timber and walk at a gentle grade along the narrow top of the lateral moraine — the term for the rubble deposited along the sides of glaciers. Farther on you'll have your first closeup views of the lowest crevasses. The glacier side of the moraine is obviously extremely unstable — don't even think of sliding down it to the equally potentially dangerous ice.

At 1.9 miles where you come to the end of the use path along the moraine veer right and begin traversing methodically along the rock face, aiming for the lowest point on the rim above. Don't think you would have had an easier time by taking the higher ridge just to the northwest either on the way in (or on the return) — these Langille Crags have spires to negotiate and some exposure.

At the crest turn left and begin the easy cross country portion of the hike. Pass cliffy outcroppings on your left, traverse along the west side of a little rounded peak — don't go to its summit — and head toward an obvious saddle. Beyond it you'll most likely be on a snowfield (unless you're doing the hike very late and the snowpack has been exceptionally low). Follow up the wide white swath to the highest rocks on the left. Bear slightly left and walk — probably along exposed rock and ground — to the viewpoint above the ice. In addition to the mesmerizing glacial view you'll be able to see Cloud Cap and more distant landmarks including The Dalles and John Day Dams. During the stroll back down along the moraine you'll spot Laurance Lake below to the north (see No. 34).

Eliot Glacier overlook

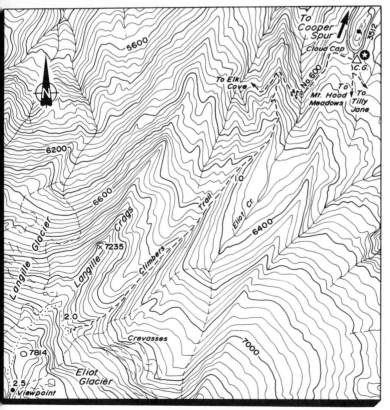

36 LAMBERSON SPUR LOOP

One day trip
Distance: 16 miles round trip
Elevation gain: 4,100 feet
High point: 6,750 feet
Allow 8 to 9 hours round trip
Usually open late July through mid October
Topographic maps:
  U.S.G.S. Badger Lake, Oreg.
  7.5′   1962
  U.S.G.S. Cathedral Ridge, Oreg.
  7.5′   1962
  U.S.G.S. Dog River, Oreg.
  7.5′   1962
  U.S.G.S. Mt. Hood South, Oreg.
  7.5′   1962

The spectacularly scenic Lamberson Spur loop on the east side of Mt. Hood is the most challenging in this guide, both physically and, because of the mile plus of faint tread and 2.0 miles of cross-country, mentally. Do this hike only in perfect weather — an especially good time is in September because the snow will be at a minimum. Hikers who want to save 4.0 miles can do so by establishing a car shuttle. Begin with water as the first source isn't until 6.2 miles.

Proceed on Oregon 35 for 16.5 miles east and north of its junction with US 26 to a turnout and a large trail sign on the east side of the highway just before the junction of the road to Cooper Spur and Cloud Cap. (To establish a shuttle, first turn left off Oregon 35 at the sign pointing to the lower ski area for Mt. Hood Meadows 8.0 miles from US 26, immediately curve left and in 0.3 mile come to trailhead parking.)

Cross Oregon 35 from the big sign to a trail that traverses up the slope, switch back and in 100 feet come to a junction (see No. 37). Turn right, after about 200 yards stay left at a signed spur and at 1.3 miles stay straight (right) on the crest. Farther on keep on the main trail where a spur heads right and then at 2.2 miles, 25 feet before a Wilderness bulletin board, come to the signed Lamberson Spur Trail. Turn right onto it and soon cross a road. Wind up to an open crest and generally continue the same way you were heading — don't veer off to the right — and resume traveling on an obvious tread. Farther on at a second, smaller but lusher open area make a semi-traverse — don't actually turn upslope but do bear right a couple of times. Beyond this section again travel on an obvious tread. At a little crest head downhill to a clearing. Bear slightly left and go through a small area of blowdown. Immediately beyond it veer right and pick up the trail. Resume mostly climbing in woods for about 0.5 mile until you're on an openish, southeast facing grassy slope where the ridge crest is above you on the right and the tread ends. The cross country begins here but the trickiest route finding is over.

Turn right, climb to the crest and turn left. Soon begin walking on the level then where the ridge resumes climbing veer left so you're on the south side of the rise and climb back to the crest. Continue along the more open ridge top, which soon becomes narrow and rocky. Periodically, you'll need to detour off the crest and, eventually, it's easier to leave the crest entirely on its left (southeast) side and walk up the swale that parallels the ridge.

Where the trees become more widely spaced veer slightly left as you continue climbing and come to a stream. Continue bearing very slightly left as you climb so you enter and travel up several adjacent side canyons. Have your first view of the Timberline Trail and where you finally reach it turn left and begin descending. Near 8.4 miles enter woods of large trees and lush little meadows and at 9.1 miles come to the junction of the trail down to Elk Meadows.

Turn left and after 0.3 mile come to a fork. If you're doing the hike as a shuttle, stay right, follow No. 652 to a four-way junction, turn right and take No. 645 out to the parking area. If you're making the loop, stay straight (left), and stay left again at the junction of the westerly trail around Elk Meadows. Cross a small stream at the northeast edge of the vast meadow, keep left, 30 feet farther stay left again on Trail No. 645 and follow it back to your starting point.

Hikers along snow covered portion of Timberline Trail

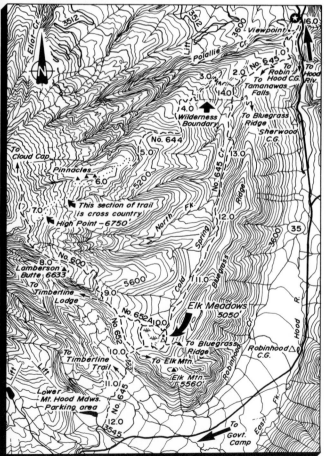

37 EAST FORK TRAIL

One day trip
Distance: 6 miles one way
Elevation gain: 150 feet, loss 800 feet
High point: 3,550 feet
Allow 2½ to 3 hours one way
Usually open late May through mid October
Topographic maps:
  U.S.G.S. Badger Lake, Oreg.
  7.5'   1962
  U.S.G.S. Dog River, Oreg.
  7.5'   1962

The gently graded 6.0 mile trail paralleling the East Fork of the Hood River is an especially good choice for a less than perfect day because, as with most river walks, there are no far ranging views. The woods along the route, especially those on the northern third, are particularly attractive in fall when the profuse vine maple turn red and gold and the scattered larch trees a luminescent yellow. The trip is perfect for a car shuttle and when done that way, like the hike to Little Crater Lake (No. 38), is ideal for a muggy or hot day when bodies want a stroll, not a strenuous workout. A side loop at the north end follows lovely Cold Spring Creek to Tamanawas Falls. For a shorter trip you could begin (or end) from the access point north of Sherwood Campground.

From the junction of US 26 and Oregon 35 drive east and north on the latter 11 miles to Robin Hood Forest Camp on the west side of the highway. If you're making the hike early or late in the season and the campground is closed, park off the highway near the entrance — don't block the gate. To establish a car shuttle, first continue with both vehicles on Oregon 35 for another 5.5 miles to a large trail sign and parking area off the east shoulder near Polallie Creek just before (south of) the junction of the Cooper Spur Road. (The middle access point is 4.2 miles north of Robin Hood Forest Camp and 1.3 miles south of the Polallie Creek end and is identified by a sign stating East Fork Trail. Cross the footbridge over the East Fork and in a few yards come to the junction of the East Fork Trail.)

Drive (or walk) into Robin Hood Forest Camp and follow the one-way loop to the signed beginning of Trail No. 650. If you're on foot, you can stay left at the beginning of the loop. Travel at a mostly gentle downhill grade along an initially wide tread. Cross a road at 1.0 mile and beyond it begin watching for larch trees, those whispy conifers whose needles turn color and drop every autumn. At 2.0 miles come to a stream. If the log over it seems too narrow, go upstream a couple of yards for a less gymnastic crossing. Near 2.3 miles climb and travel above a slide area. Just beyond where you glimpse a road above on your left the trail drops back to river level. Farther on make a considerably shorter climb and descent and then travel across from Sherwood Forest Camp. As you walk along a narrow, natural dike note the mix of wee firs, pines, cedars and larches. Abruptly, the woods become more attractive — lusher and tidier.

At the junction of the middle access trail stay left and continue north past more vine maple and then climb briefly. As you curve into the side canyon holding Cold Spring Creek look across the highway and up to a fine example of columnar basalt. Traverse down to a junction. The most direct route to the end of the hike is to turn right, descend to Cold Spring Creek, cross it on a bridge, climb out of the side canyon and then traverse in a series of short up, down and level stretches.

Although there's nothing unattractive about the short way out, even better (but 1.5 miles longer) is to stay straight at the junction at 4.9 miles. Descend a short distance to a higher bridge over Cold Spring Creek, cross it and hike parallel to the flow for 0.9 mile and switch back. At a second turn come to the 0.2 mile spur to Tamanawas Falls. After a visit to it resume climbing to a junction at the crest of the ridge (see No. 36). Turn right, wind down, passing the short spur to the Polallie Creek Overlook, to the junction with the shorter route. Turn left and walk the final couple hundred feet to the highway.

Trail sign near Sherwood Campground

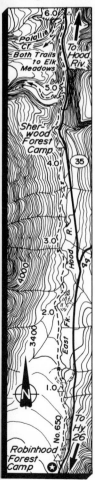

38 WAPINITIA PASS to LITTLE CRATER LAKE

One day trip
Distance: 7.7 miles one way
Elevation gain: 300 feet; loss 1,100 feet
High point: 4,200 feet
Allow 3 to 3½ hours one way
Usually open June through early November
Topographic maps:
  U.S.G.S. High Rock, Oreg.
  15'   1956
  U.S.G.S. Mt. Wilson, Oreg.
  15'   1956

Because of the abundance of access points, hikers so inclined could do almost the entire Pacific Crest Trail through Oregon as day hikes. One such possibility is the gently graded portion of the PCT between Wapinitia Pass and Little Crater Lake that travels through woods that are surprisingly varied in their makeup, considering the short distance and modest change in elevation. The southernmost end of the hike is in a vast meadow that affords a view of Mt. Hood and, at times, herds of grazing cattle.

Although it doesn't much resemble its namesake, Little Crater Lake with its sheer sides and unique blue color doesn't resemble any other lake, either. As with most segments along the PCT, the hike is perfect for a car shuttle. The only water source is from the spring at the midway point.

From the junction of US 26 and Oregon 35 head south on US 26, as if you were going to Bend, for 4.7 miles to the road that heads left to a huge parking area and Frog Lake Campground. This is where you'll begin the hike. To establish a shuttle, continue with both cars on US 26 for another 4.2 miles to Skyline Road 42. Turn right onto it and after 4.0 miles turn right on Road 58, following the signs to Little Crater Lake and High Rock. In 2.5 miles turn left onto Road 230 to Little Crater Lake Campground. If you do this hike early or late in the season, the large campground sign might not be installed. After 0.2 mile keep right and continue to the parking turnouts for the trail to Little Crater Lake. Return with the second car to the parking area near Frog Lake.

From the north side of the parking lot walk several yards to a T-junction with the PCT, turn left, cross the highway and continue in the same direction. After a couple of hundred feet come to the junction of a trail to Clear Lake. Stay right (straight) and traverse moderately uphill through deep woods. After about 1.8 miles begin an equally moderate descent. Except for a few brief climbs and several level stretches, the remainder of the hike is gradually downhill. Around 2.0 miles pass near the first of two clearcuts. At 3.2 miles an abandoned route angles back to the right and a short distance farther the make up of the woods changes abruptly to lodgepole pine. At a little sign on your right listing 4.0 miles back to Wapinitia Pass and 4.0 miles ahead to Little Crater Lake look left off the trail for a campsite, which is a perfect place for a lunch stop. To locate the spring here head southwest for several yards from the campfire area.

Three-tenths mile beyond the camp the trail crosses the road and 0.6 mile farther it crosses a second one. Come to a final road at 6.4 miles and veer right as you cross it to find the trail. Follow a circuitous, level route through the woods of widely spaced, stately old trees for 0.9 mile to a sign pointing left to Trail 500. In 1984 this area was logged using horses to drag away the felled trees. The PCT continues south and reaches Timothy Lake (No. 45) in less than a mile.

To complete the hike to Little Crater Lake, turn left onto Trail No. 500. Come to the edge of the meadow and walk along a boardwalk. Climb a stile over a pole fence and meet the lake where plaques explain its formation. Follow the path through a finger of woods, cross another stile and walk through more meadow to the trailhead.

Little Crater Lake

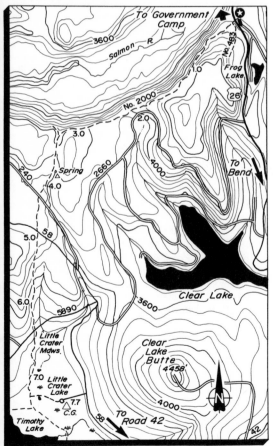

39   SQUAW MOUNTAIN

One day trip
Distance: 2.8 miles one way
Elevation gain: 950 feet, loss 350 feet
High point: 4,771 feet
Allow 1½ hours one way
Usually open late June through mid October
Topographic map:
  U.S.G.S. Fish Creek Mtn., Oreg.
  15′   1956

The trail to Squaw Mountain skirts the southernmost corner of the new (1984) Salmon-Huckleberry Wilderness. In addition to an overview of the preserve, the scene from the summit includes Mounts Hood and Jefferson, Silver Star in Washington, Larch Mountain on the Oregon side of the Columbia Gorge, terrain comprising the Clackamas River drainage and the less wild country around Estacada, Portland and the Columbia River. The trip to Salmon Mountain (No. 40) begins from the same trailhead.

Drive southeast of Estacada on Oregon 224 for 7.5 miles to a road on your left across from the entrance to a commercial marina on North Fork Reservoir. Turn left, following the sign pointing to North Fork Crossing, Twin Springs and other destinations, and immediately turn left again onto unpaved Road 4610. After 7.4 miles keep left, still on 4610, and then 0.9 mile farther stay right on 4610, still following the signs to Twin Springs. Continue on 4610 for 10.5 miles to a sign on your left stating Plaza Trail No. 783. This trailhead is 100 feet before the signed entrance to Twin Springs Campground.

From the road walk 75 feet north to a T-junction and turn left. (The route to the right is the Plaza Trail that passes the spur to Salmon Mountain and continues north to Huckleberry Mountain (see No. 32).) For the initial 1.8 miles the Squaw Mountain Trail alternates between level and moderately graded up or down stretches. Parallel the road for a bit and then curve right and travel through lusher woods. At 0.8 mile cross to the south side of the ridge, farther on come to an open, rocky section where you can see down over a meadow filled valley holding the Squaw Lakes, which you passed on the drive to the trailhead. This basin is a perfect example of a common natural progression: Not so very long ago, shallow lakes probably covered considerably more of the valley floor. As inlet streams deposited sediments, plants began to take hold. If conditions continue to be favorable, vegetation eventually will take over the valley. And, if the ground is well drained, trees will begin encroaching on the meadow, filling in the open areas just as the grasses and shrubs replaced the lakes. Certainly not all lakes meet this fate nor were all meadows formed in this manner, but it is a common pattern. Squaw Mountain is visible ahead to the west but you'll probably be more certain of its precise location after you've come back from the summit.

At 1.2 miles cross a deeply wooded saddle and then resume traversing along the south side of the ridge. Begin a steady climb at about 1.8 miles and then wind up in several switchbacks past many huckleberry and rhododendron bushes and attendant clumps of beargrass. In early July you'll enjoy the flowers and in August the berries. Come to a T-junction at a saddle where an old enamel sign marks former trails to Cache Meadow and the Roaring River. The route down to the right goes out to Old Baldy and down to Eagle Creek.

Turn left, continue uphill, switch back once and travel along the north facing slope to a road, which, unfortunately, has not been closed to vehicles. Turn left, follow the road as it curves right and just before its end take the path up to the summit, the site of a former fire lookout cabin. Less familiar landmarks include Signal Buttes, Dry Ridge, the terrain comprising the drainage of the Roaring River and Goat and Fish Creek Mountains. Devils Peak (see No. 33), Hunchback Ridge, Salmon Butte and Wildcat and Huckleberry Mountains are highpoints in the Salmon-Huckleberry Wilderness.

Old lookout foundation

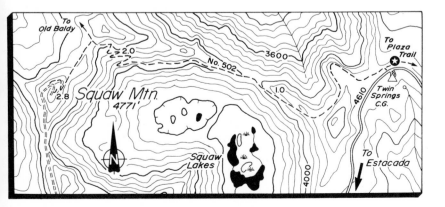

40 SALMON MOUNTAIN

One day trip
Distance: 5 miles one way
Elevation gain: 500 feet, loss 750 feet
High point: 4,600 feet
Allow 3 hours one way
Usually open late June through mid October
Topographic map:
   U.S.G.S. Fish Creek Mtn., Oreg.
   15'   1956

Salmon Mountain is about 3.5 miles northwest of its considerably better known neighbor Salmon Butte. Both share far-ranging views that include Mounts Hood, Adams, Rainier and St. Helens. Not to denigrate the route to Salmon Butte, but most hikers would agree that the one to Salmon Mountain is even more interesting. The latter's trail passes a couple of impressive, rocky viewpoints, traverses brushy slopes that remind the visitor of the northen Washington Cascades and for the final mile is along a rustic tread — in fact, the last 100 yards is cross-country. Begin with adequate water in case the small streams near the midway point aren't flowing.

Proceed southeast of Estacada on Oregon 224 for 7.5 miles to a road on your left across from the entrance to a commercial marina on North Fork Reservoir. Turn left, following the sign pointing to North Fork Crossing, Twin Springs and other destinations, and immediately turn left again onto unpaved Road 4610. After 7.4 miles keep left, still on 4610, and then 0.9 mile farther stay right on 4610, still following the signs to Twin Springs. Continue on 4610 for 10.5 miles to a sign on your left stating Plaza Trail No. 783. This trailhead is 100 feet before the signed entrance to Twin Springs Campground.

From the road walk 75 feet north to a T-junction and turn right. (The route to the left goes to Squaw Mountain (No. 39).) Soon begin climbing gradually and near 0.5 mile come to a section of an old road. Keep left along it and after several yards veer left again onto the signed Plaza Trail. The ruins on your left are of the Plaza Guard Station. You'll be traveling in the new (1984) 44,600 acre Salmon-Huckleberry Wilderness for the entire hike. At 1.0 mile begin descending and after about 0.2 mile pass a path on your right to a viewpoint. For an even better overlook, continue along the main trail a short distance farther to a large sign marking the path to Sheeps Head Rock Viewpoint. The terrain you'll look over from this knobby outcropping includes the timbered slopes that feed the South Fork of the Salmon River and, to the west, the valley that holds Eagle Creek.

Just beyond the spur to the viewpoint descend in two sets of switchbacks and then have a brief uphill and level stretch before resuming the downhill. Curve around the nose of a ridge and traverse along a brushy slope, crossing a few little streams. Re-enter woods and at 3.3 miles come to the signed Salmon Mountain Trail on your right. The main route continues north past Huckleberry Mountain (see No. 32).

Turn right and climb very steeply for about 150 yards and then begin descending. After a section of roller coaster grades walk along the crest for about 200 feet to where the path veers off to the left (north). Don't worry about missing this deviation because about 70 feet farther along the crest you'll come to a steep, rubbly section topped by narrow rock outcroppings. Traverse down along the north side of the ridge and then climb back to the crest. Follow along the south side for a couple hundred feet and then again drop along the north side on a rooty tread and climb back to the crest. Turn right here at the crest, leaving the faint tread, and traverse uphill cross country on the southeast facing slope for the final 100 yards to the site of the former lookout cabin. From the crest the trail, such as it is, continues down for several miles through a jungle of rhododendrons and eventually dies in an old clearcut.

Phlox along trail

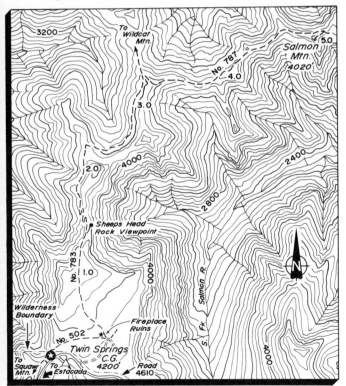

41 MEMALOOSE LAKE and SOUTH FORK MOUNTAIN

One day trip or short backpack
Distance: 1.5 miles to Memaloose Lake;
0.8 mile additional to South Fork Mountain
Elevation gain: 550 feet to Memaloose Lake; 750 feet additional to South Fork Mountain
High point: 4,853 feet
Allow ¾ hour to Memaloose Lake; ½ hour additional to South Fork Mountain
Usually open late June through October
Topographic map:
U.S.G.S. Fish Creek Mtn., Oreg.
15′   1956

The moderately graded climb through an old growth forest to Memaloose Lake is a satisfying trip for hikers who want an easy outing but people with a bit more energy are encouraged to continue winding uphill for the extra 0.8 mile to enjoy the panorama from the summit of South Fork Mountain. Just being

able to see the major peaks from Mt. Rainier to the Three Sisters would be noteworthy enough but the view also includes the Willamette Valley south to near Salem, the Coast Range and, most exceptional, the buildings of downtown Portland.

From Estacada head southeast on Oregon 224 (the Upper Clackamas River Road) 9.8 miles, passing the North Fork Reservoir, to signs identifying the Memaloose Road and giving mileages to the lake. Turn right and cross a bridge over the Clackamas River. You're now on Road 45 and will be staying on it all the way to the trailhead. After 10.8 miles from the bridge come to a final junction, where the pavement ends, keep right on 45 and in 0.8 mile be watching for a small sign on your left identifying the start of the Memaloose Lake Trail.

Traverse uphill parallel to the road and then descend slightly to an unsigned trail on your right. Note the junction so you don't inadvertently follow this abandoned route on your return. It goes back to the road but the alignment is through some swampy terrain. Many old routes are fun to follow but this is one that isn't. Hop a couple of small streams and then a slightly larger one. After four switchbacks cross yet another stream, the last easily accessible source of potable water. Travel near Memaloose Creek and after another series of switchbacks, cross it. Traverse up, curve left and walk at a levelish grade to relatively shallow, five acre Memaloose Lake. Good campsites are above the south shore near a small inlet creek.

To reach the summit of South Fork Mountain continue along the east side of the lake on the main trail, recross Memaloose Creek and soon resume climbing. Curve left, switch back right where an old route heads left and meander uphill. Have three more switchbacks and then travel through a short section where the tread is faint. However, blazes abundantly mark this stretch and you'll have no trouble staying on course. Return to an obvious tread and continue winding up to a ridge crest. Walk along its top, traverse below it for a bit and then make the final few short switchbacks to the summit, the site of a former fire lookout tower.

Beyond the immediate ring of clearcuts you'll see, in addition to the major peaks and Portland, Saddle Mountain (No. 7), the high point in the northern part of the Coast Range, and even taller Marys Peak farther south in the chain. The highpoint close-in to the northwest with the lookout tower is Goat Mountain. Table Rock (No. 46) is the hulk to the south and the Bull of the Woods Wilderness (see No's. 47, 48 and 49) is a bit farther to the southeast.

Memaloose Lake

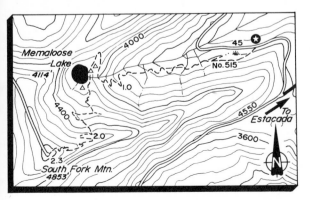

42 CLACKAMAS RIVER TRAIL

One day trip
Distance: 7.5 miles one way
Elevation gain: 600 feet; loss 200 feet
High point: 1,400 feet
Allow 4 to 4½ hours one way
Usually open February through December
Topographic map:
U.S.G.S. Fish Creek Mtn., Oreg.
15′   1956

Completed in 1981, the 7.5 mile route that parallels the Clackamas River between Fish Creek and Indian Henry Campgrounds is brand new, not a reopening of a long abandoned route. As on most hikes along creeks and rivers, you'll be impressed by how many personalities water can possess. And the vegetation is almost as varied, from the predominant Douglas fir to huge cedars, alder, vine maple, grassy slopes and even meadows.

Because there are no far ranging views, the Clackamas River Trail is a good choice for a gloomy, or even a rainy, day and with its low elevation is hikeable later into the fall or earlier in the spring. The trip is perfect for a car shuttle and, considering the length, just about requires one.

From Estacada proceed southeast on Oregon 224 beside the Clackamas River for 16.2 miles to the junction on your right just beyond Fish Creek Campground of Road 54 to Fish Creek and Surprise Lake. If you're doing the trip using a car shuttle, hiking either direction is satisfactory but the route is a bit more interesting heading upstream. So, assuming you're intending to establish a shuttle and hike from north to south, continue with both cars on Oregon 224 another 6.9 miles to the sign just before a bridge on 224 identifying Sandstone Road No. 4620 to Indian Henry Campground. Keep right on Sandstone Road and after 0.6 mile come to the entrance to Indian Henry Campground. The south end of the Clackamas River Trail begins across the road opposite the entrance. If the campground is open you can turn left into it and park in the turnout on your right on the far side of the bridge. To complete the shuttle, return to Road 54 to Fish and Surprise Lake. Turn left, immediately cross a bridge and park in the large open space on your right just beyond the span.

Cross 54 to the possibly unsigned, but obvious, trail that begins from the southeast corner of the bridge. After about 250 feet come to a scenic old road, turn left and follow it for 0.2 mile or so to its end and the resumption of the trail proper. The route alternates among traveling near water level or traversing well above the river and being close to the flow or a bit inland. Occasionally, you'll be reminded that Oregon 224 is across the river but, overall, the highway isn't too intrusive. Near 2.1 miles pass a campsite and continue climbing and decending for another 1.0 mile to the edge of a huge cleared swath under power lines. Pass through a lovely grove of alder to the crossing of Pup Creek, which, as with all the streams along the hike, is no problem to ford, and then walk the length of an immense meadow.

Re-enter woods with an elegant ambience of widely spaced conifers. Eventually begin traversing uphill, cross a small stream and then lose the elevation just gained. At a spur on your left keep right on the main trail and farther on come to an outcropping of knobby rocks where you'll have a view down onto The Narrows. There's no potable water here but the grassy ledge is otherwise perfect for a food stop. To visit the ledge, descend along the main trail from the overlook, switchback and then at the second turn don't make it but instead leave the trail and head in the same direction.

Near 5.2 miles cross a good sized stream and farther on traverse under an eroded, overhanging rock that resembles a formation you'd see in the Columbia Gorge. After a bit more uphill walk on the level and at an openish area have a view of the surge tank for the Three Lynx powerhouse. Descend some, cross a bridge over a deep side canyon and hike the final 0.9 mile to the south end of the trail.

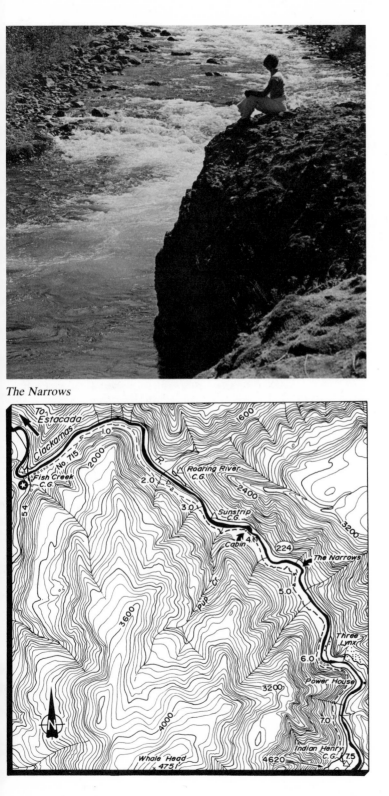

The Narrows

43 RIVERSIDE TRAIL

One day trip
Distance: 4 miles one way
Elevation gain: 300 feet; loss 200 feet
High point: 1,450 feet
Allow 2½ hours one way
Usually open March through December
Topographic map:
  U.S.G.S. Fish Creek Mtn., Oreg.
  15'   1956

Unlike the new (1981) Clackamas River Trail (No. 42) that parallels the west bank, the Riverside Trail, several miles upstream and on the other side of the river, was constructed around 1915. This older route once extended from Estacada to Olallie Lake but today clearcuts, roads and abandonment have combined to leave only the 4.0 mile section between Rainbow and Riverside Campgrounds intact.

As with most river walks, the Riverside Trail is a particularly good choice for earlier in the spring or later in the fall when higher routes aren't snow-free and on a gloomy or wet day any time during the hiking season. Also, it's perfect for a car shuttle. Like No's. 37 and 38, the Riverside Trail is just right when you crave some exercise and fresh air but don't want to work too hard.

From Estacada drive southeast on Oregon 224 for 27 miles to a fork 0.5 mile beyond the Ripplebrook Ranger Station. Turn right on Road 46 and in a short distance come to the entrance on your right of Rainbow Campground. If you're establishing a shuttle, continue with both cars along 46 for another 3.0 miles to Riverside Campground, leave one vehicle here and return with the other to Rainbow Campground. (If the campgrounds are closed, park near the entrances, being sure not to block the gates.) There's no reason you couldn't do the hike from south to north — it's just that river walks seem to be a bit more interesting going upstream.

At Rainbow Campground drive (or walk) down the entrance road and continue to the far end of the loop where a large sign stating Job Corps Conservation Project identifies the beginning of the trail.

As is typical of routes that follow rivers, the Riverside Trail doesn't hug the edge of the flow and climb at a steady, gentle grade but, instead, is a series of short up, down and level stretches. Frequently, the alignment is well away from the sight of water. Several hundred feet from the trailhead walk beside the Oak Grove Fork for a short distance and then begin paralleling the Clackamas River proper. On the sections of the hike that travel directly above the river you may be entertained by kayakers, rafters and other boaters bobbing downstream. The tread is a bit faint for a few yards a couple of times near the beginning but the general alignment is reasonably obvious, so you should have no trouble re-finding the well defined tread.

Tag Creek at 1.9 miles may be missigned as Tar Creek, which you'll actually be crossing at 3.7 miles. Beyond yet another uphill stretch pass a large rock outcropping and then travel near an area of slippage, the second so far along the hike. River walks offer particularly good opportunities to observe examples of the basic instability of land. Come to a more open area, cross two faint cat roads, have a view northwest to Fish Creek Mountain, the destination of a 2.1 mile hike, and re-enter woods. Where you begin a descent, you can see north to Dry Ridge, up which wends a considerably longer, more demanding trail.

As you come near the highway where a trail heads right stay left and switch back. Travel parallel to Road 46 and then walk along a grassy shelf. Follow an old road, still paralleling 46, cross a spur coming in from the highway and resume hiking on a trail. Eventually, veer away from 46 and walk right against the water's edge. Have one last climb and descent before coming to Riverside Campground.

Footbridge

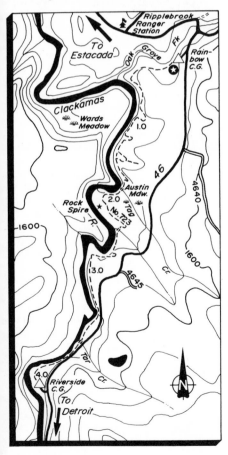

44 SHINING LAKE

One day trip or short backpack
Distance: 4.7 miles one way
Elevation gain: 250 feet; loss 800 feet
High point: 4,820 feet
Allow 2 hours one way
Usually open July through October
Topographic maps:
U.S.G.S. Fish Creek Mtn., Oreg.
15' 1956
U.S.G.S. High Rock, Oreg.
15' 1956

If the weather cooperates by being warm the second half of August, the trip to Shining Lake offers a chance to pick (and eat) huckleberries and also to go swimming. Earlier in the summer, around the first part of July, you'll be delighted by the blooms of rhododendrons and on any clear day throughout the hiking season you'll enjoy views of Mounts Adams, Rainier and Hood and highpoints in the Columbia Gorge. Note that most of the climbing is done on the return. Begin with adequate water.

Although the approach to the trailhead is a bit circuitous, the drive is scenically interesting, with the final portion over less familiar terrain. From Estacada head southeast on Oregon 224 for 27 miles to a junction 0.5 beyond the Ripplebrook Ranger Station. Turn left onto Road 57 and after 7.2 miles keep left on 58. Continue on 58, which is paved for 5.1 miles, 6.8 miles to a junction where two roads go left and take the upper one, 4610. To the right here is High Rock, a landmark often seen from summits in the Salmon-Huckleberry Wilderness and other high points just south of Mt. Hood. After 1.2 miles keep left on 240 and follow it 4.1 miles to the junction of 250. (If you stayed left here, you'd shortly come to the beginning of the trails to Serene Lake, Cache Meadow and other destinations.) To reach Shining Lake, however, stay right on Road 270 and drive uphill a few hundred feet to a small picnic area and park here.

Walk gradually downhill along the road, pass a locked gate and then climb a short distance to a view of Mounts Hood and Adams and, farther on, Rainier. Salmon Butte, Hunchback Ridge (No. 33) and West Zigzag Mountain are highpoints between you and Mt. Hood and Tanner Butte and Mt. Defiance (No. 27) are two of the most obvious landmarks in the Columbia Gorge. Eventually, you'll be able to look southwest to Dry Ridge on your left, one of the several massive ridges that form the canyons of the Roaring River and its tributaries. Continue down along the road that has such an imperceptible grade you probably won't notice it...until the return trip.

At 3.4 miles begin traveling through more open terrain and come to an old sign marking Shining Lake Forest Camp. Turn right and follow the spur about 100 yards to a sign at the rim of the basin where you can peer down over Shining Lake. If you're planning a swim, locate the one brush-free area at the north end of the lake as this is about the only spot where you can easily reach the shore.

Wind down along a trail in five switchbacks. Where the trail forks keep right and contour above the east shoreline. A good stopping place for non-swimmers is in a grassy area above the northeast side of the lake.

Camp sign near Shining Lake

45 TIMOTHY LAKE

One day trip
Distance: 11.2 miles round trip
Elevation gain: 300 feet round trip
High point: 3,280 feet
Allow 5 to 6 hours round trip
Usually open late May through mid
November
Topographic map:
U.S.G.S. High Rock, Oreg.
15'   1956

In addition to providing ever-changing views across the expanse of water to the opposite shoreline, the trail around Timothy Lake travels through a variety of woods, skirts several large meadows and provides a glimpse of Mt. Jefferson and many perspectives of Mt. Hood. The hike can be made shorter by establishing a car shuttle and ending at Little Crater Lake (No. 38) or Oak Fork Campground. If you're making the loop during summer be warned that the final 2.5 miles along the south shore passes several large, popular campgrounds.

From Estacada head southeast on Oregon 224 for 27 miles to a junction 0.5 mile beyond the Ripplebrook Ranger Station and keep left on Road 57, as indicated by the sign pointing to Timothy Lake and

US 26. After 2.7 miles come to a junction. If you stay straight on 57 you'll save 2.0 miles of driving but you'll be on an unpaved road. To go the longer, paved, way bear left on 58, after 1.0 mile turn right onto 5810 and take it 8.5 miles to the junction with 57. Turn left and in 0.1 mile, just before the road crosses the dam, turn left and park in one of the spaces between the spur and the shore. To reach Timothy Lake from US 26, follow that highway 8.9 miles south of its junction with Oregon 35 to the junction of Road 42, the Skyline Road. Stay on 42 for 8.5 miles then turn onto Road 57 and take it 3.5 miles to the west end of the lake.

From the parking area walk along the road for a few hundred feet to the beginning of Trail No. 528. Hike on the level through woods and at 1.3 miles, between the second and third bridges, pass the unsigned spur to Meditation Point. Farther on have that view of Mt. Jefferson. Near 2.5 miles look across the narrow neck of an inlet to the other side of the lake — there will be almost four miles of hiking before you reach that opposite shore. Have your first views of Mt. Hood and farther on walk behind a drive-in campground. Cross the campground access road and continue on the level through woods to the junction with the Pacific Crest Trail. If you've established a car shuttle at Little Crater Lake or are intending to make the short trip to it, turn left onto the PCT and after 0.2 mile turn right onto Trail No. 500.

To continue the hike around Timothy Lake turn right onto the PCT. Cross a small bridge and then a larger one that spans Crater Creek. Don't obtain drinking water from it for it is polluted by range cattle. After another section of woods pass the meadowy south side of the inlet. You may see — and what with their bells — hear those range cattle. In the Cascades, they usually don't populate the same areas hikers do, so it's a treat to encounter them. Although they're not looking for trouble, don't approach them and prevent any dogs you might have with you from doing so, too.

Travel away from the lake and then walk above it. At 8.0 miles come to a junction, turn right, leaving the PCT, and make one switchback down to a bridge. The trail is not obvious for a hundred feet or so beyond the span. Veer toward the creek and you'll be funneled onto the main route that resumes following the shoreline.

Where the trail is obscure as it passes the campgrounds just stay as close as is reasonable to the water's edge and eventually resume walking along a well defined tread. At the final, most westerly campground, however, the best route is to follow the paved road through the camp area. Where you meet Road 57 turn right, cross the dam and turn right to reach your car.

Mt. Hood from Timothy Lake

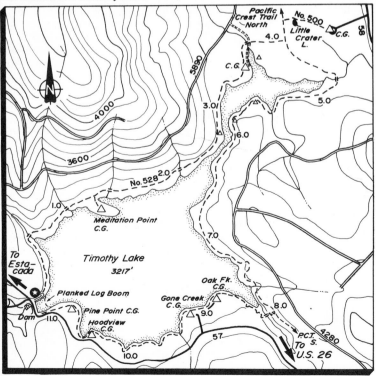

46 TABLE and ROOSTER ROCKS

One day trip
Distance: 2.3 miles one way to Table Rock;
    1.4 miles additional to Rooster
    Rock
Elevation gain: 1,280 feet to Table Rock;
    600 feet additional to
    Rooster Rock and 560 feet
    loss
High point: 4,881 feet
Allow 1½ hours one way to Table Rock;
   1 hour additional to Rooster Rock
Usually open June through October
Topographic map:
 U.S.G.S. Mill City, Oreg.
 15' 1955

The 5,500 acre Table Rock Wilderness southeast of Molalla is one of the new preserves born along with 22 others in Oregon in June, 1984. In addition to the massive outcroppings of Table and Rooster Rocks, the wilderness boasts panoramas that include every major peak, and many minor ones, from Mt. Ranier to the Three Sisters plus a look into a portion of the Willamette Valley. By establishing a car shuttle, hikers can follow the 8.8 mile L shaped trail system through the area. People who want an easier trip can end at Table Rock and still enjoy all the views.

From the center of Molalla, located about 15 miles south of Oregon City, head east on Oregon 211, as if you were going to Estacada. After 0.6 mile come to the signed junction of the route to Freyer Park and Dickey Prairie. If you're approaching on Oregon 211 from the north, this turn is 20 miles south of Estacada. Turn off 211 onto S. Mathias Road and after 0.3 mile curve left, now on Freyer Park Road. In 1.8 miles come to a T-junction just beyond a bridge and turn right onto S. Dickey Prairie Road. After 1.7 miles come to the store at Dickey Prairie and stay right, continuing on S. Dickey Prairie Road. In 3.7 miles turn right, following the main road, and cross a bridge. Three-tenths mile from the span curve left, continuing on the paved surface, and follow this road 12.5 miles to a signed junction just before a bridge. If you're establishing a car shuttle, keep right, cross the bridge and park off the left side of the road. This lower trailhead begins directly behind the sign.

To reach the upper trailhead, keep left at the junction just before the bridge onto unpaved, signed Middle Fork Road. After 2.1 miles cross the river and 0.6 mile farther come to the signed junction on your right of the Table Rock Access Road. Turn right, 2.0 miles farther keep straight (left) and drive the final 3.7 miles to the trailhead on your right, which may be unsigned but can be identified by a built-up section of tread that resembles a dirt bridge. Another fix is the cone shaped highpoint in the clearcut below the road across from the trailhead.

Meander up through woods and at 0.4 mile pass a small stream, the only source of water. Continue the moderate climb, traveling near several rock outcroppings, and at 1.0 mile leave the woods, come to a scree slope and traverse along the base of the sheer rock wall that forms the north side of Table Rock. Re-enter woods and curve around to the considerably less imposing west side of the peak. After traversing south about 0.3 mile come to a relatively open saddle and a possibly unsigned junction.

To reach Table Rock, turn left on the main route, make two switchbacks to the spiney summit and walk to its north end. Rooster Rock is on the ridge across the valley to the southwest and Bull of the Woods (No. 49) is the easterly highpoint with the barely discernible lookout.

To reach Rooster Rock, descend back to the saddle at 1.8 miles and continue to the southwest. After a brief climb travel along a crest. Although the route between Table and Rooster Rocks is not high grade, it isn't difficult to follow and sections are marked with pink surveyor's tape. Have a steepish descent to a saddle, a stretch of minor ups and downs and at 2.7 miles follow the trail as it leaves the crest on the right side. Descend to a swampy area, cross near its north side and then climb along a trail back to the ridge top at the base of Rooster Rock.

If you've established a shuttle, head northwest along the ridge. Even if you're not doing the hike one way, you're urged to head northwest from Rooster Rock at least for a few tenths mile. The slopes of ground hugging heather and kinnikinnick with scattered rock outcroppings and small conifers simulate a high alpine scene found nowhere else in this wilderness.

118

Aerial view of Table Rock

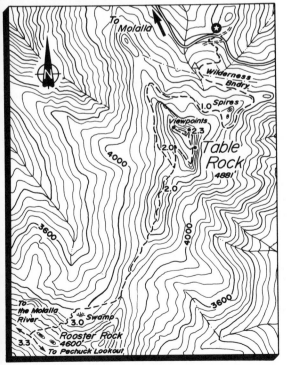

47 WHETSTONE MOUNTAIN and SILVER KING LAKE

One day trip or backpack
Distance: 4.7 miles one way to Silver King Lake; 1.1 miles additional to Whetstone Mountain
Elevation gain: 910 feet; loss 800 feet to Silver King Lake; 850 feet additional gain to Whetstone Mountain
High point: 4,969 feet
Allow 3 hours to Silver King Lake; ¾ hour additional to Whetstone Mountain
Usually open mid June through October
Topographic map:
U.S.G.S. Battle Ax, Oreg.
15′   1956

Even if the view from Whetstone Mountain didn't include sightings of Three Fingered Jack, Mt. Washington and all three of the Sisters plus Mounts Adams, Hood and Jefferson, hiking farther into the westernmost portion of the new (1984) Bull of the Woods Wilderness to Silver King Lake would be exceptional because the open ridge between 3.0 and 4.0 miles has an ambience uncommon to the northern Oregon Cascades. Not as exotic, but certainly noteworthy, is the jungle of rhododendrons around 1.5 miles, which put on their blooming show near the first part of July, and the old growth forests along the first and final thirds of the hike.

Although you could hike only to Whetstone Mountain or Silver King Lake, you're urged to do both

because each place is too good to miss. The lake would be a good spot for a base camp from which to make day hikes north to Bagby Hot Springs or south to Battle Ax, Twin Lakes and other points. Start with adequate water, particularly later in the season when the one stream near 1.0 mile may not be flowing.

From Estacada head southeast on Oregon 224 for 27 miles to a fork 0.5 mile beyond the Ripplebrook Ranger Station and keep right on Road 46. In 3.7 miles keep right on Road 63 and after 3.6 miles come to the junction of Road 70. Turn right onto it, still following signs to Bagby Hot Springs. After 6.6 miles pass a sign on your left marking the trail to the hot springs and 0.9 mile farther along 70 come to the junction of 7020 on your left and the end of the pavement.

Keep straight (right) and after 1.8 miles turn left onto oiled 7030, following the sign pointing to Whetstone Mountain Trail. In 5.7 miles come to another junction with 7020 and turn right. After 0.7 mile veer left onto a road that heads down to a flat, cleared area. Don't worry about missing this spur because 7020 ends in less than 0.5 mile. After the hike you could follow 7020 back to 70 instead of turning on 7030. This optional return is 1.4 miles shorter but it's unpaved.

The trail begins from the south side of the flat area. Descend and cross the clearcut to the deep timber and then follow a circuitous route that alternates between level and uphill stretches for 1.4 miles to the junction of the trail to Whetstone Mountain.

To visit the peak, turn right and after traversing, with one set of switchbacks, come to a signed fork and wind up for 0.2 mile to the rocky summit. You can see the ridge you'll be traversing farther along the hike and just beyond it is the summit of Battle Ax. Among the plethora of landmarks are Bull of the Woods (No. 49) to the east and Table and Rooster Rocks (No. 46) to the northwest.

Retrace your route to the junction at 1.4 miles, turn right and head east past those robust rhodies. Descend gradually and after a level stretch resume climbing. Keep left at a junction at 1.8 miles and continue up to a narrow ridge crest. One of the many charms of this hike is the ever-changing scenery and vegetation. So, if you're not taken with one stretch another more to your liking probably will be coming up shortly.

After two pairs of switchbacks travel across an open, rocky slope and at 4.0 miles come to the junction of the trail to Elk Lake. Turn left, and wind down for 0.9 mile. One hundred feet from where you bottom out at a little clearing and as you re-enter woods look for a signed trail on your left that climbs for 0.2 mile to Silver King Lake.

Rhododendrons in bloom

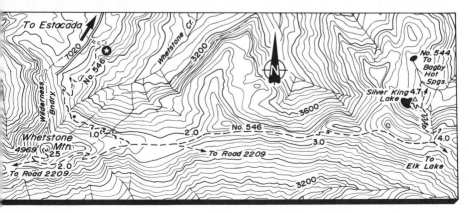

48 DICKEY CREEK TRAIL

One day trip or backpack
Distance: 5 miles one way to Big Slide Lake
Elevation gain: 1,600 feet; loss 250 feet
High point: 4,200 feet
Allow 3 hours one way
Usually open mid June through October
Topographic map:
   U.S.G.S. Battle Ax, Oreg.
   15′   1956

The Dickey Creek Trail in the north central portion of the new (1984) Bull of the Woods Wilderness is one of those routes that has something for everyone. People out just for a day hike will find Big Slide Lake at 5.0 miles a good stopping point. Those who want a bit more exercise and exceptionally far ranging views can continue up for another 1.5 miles, with an elevation gain of 1,300 feet, to the lookout on the summit of Bull of the Woods (No. 49). Backpackers can establish a base camp at Big Slide Lake and make day hikes to Welcome Lakes, Big Slide Mountain, Twin Lakes and Pansy Basin, to cite only four of the many possible destinations. To further increase its versatility, the Dickey Creek Trail is equally scenic on either a cloudy or a clear day, assuming you're not heading up to Bull of the Woods for the panorama. Many thousand rhodo-dendron bushes line the route, especially between the 3.0 and 4.5 mile points, and they are at their blooming best around the end of June. It would be impossible to decide whether the scene created by these masses of pink amidst the greens of the forest is more exquisite in misty or in sunny weather. Hikers who want to establish a short car shuttle could return along Trail No. 550 (see No. 49).

Proceed southeast of Estacada on Oregon 224 for 27 miles to a fork 0.5 mile beyond the Ripplebrook Ranger Station. Stay right on Road 46, following the sign to Bagby Hot Springs, and after 3.7 miles keep right on Road 63. After 5.7 miles along Road 63 keep right on Road 6340, as indicated by signs to the Dickey Creek, Bull of the Woods and Pansy Basin Trails. In 2.8 miles, where the pavement ends, turn left and follow Road 140 for 1.6 miles to its end and the beginning of the signed trailhead. (If you're establishing a shuttle, you'll continue along 6340 from the junction of 140.)

Walk on the level along the blocked road and soon have a view up the valley to the lookout on Bull of the Woods. Descend steeply for 0.5 mile along the only section of poor tread of the hike. Begin winding uphill past luxuriant carpets of moss. Farther on follow a straighter course at an erratic, but never steep, uphill grade to a lush clearing near 2.0 miles. Follow the trail to a faint junction, turn left, after several yards turn right and pick your way through a swampy area for about 100 feet. Come to a small lake, where you may see evidence of beaver, and traverse above its west side.

Climb through increasingly good looking woods for 1.0 mile, crossing two small side streams, and then descend briefly to the ford of Dickey Creek. To avoid having to scramble over the rocks on the opposite bank, you can cross a bit upstream. Fill your bottle here in case the source at 4.8 miles has dried up. Traverse above the creek in a downstream direction, curve right and climb in four switchbacks. After a lengthy traverse along the valley wall make two turns and cross a more open slope. Re-enter deeper woods and eventually make two sets of short, steep switchbacks. Lose some elevation and pass an old sign pointing to a water source a couple of yards down from the trail.

Hike below scree slopes and then traverse one. Re-enter woods and about 0.1 mile beyond the rocks be watching for a possibly unsigned path heading steeply downhill on your right. This is the route to Big Slide Lake. The best camping is on the west side near the north and south ends. The main trail continues up to a junction at the rim of the basin where one route heads east to Welcome Lakes and Big Slide Mountain and another goes south to connectors to Bull of the Woods, Pansy Basin and Twin Lakes.

lder tree felled by beavers

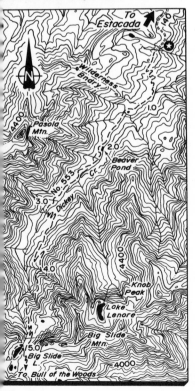

49 BULL of the WOODS

One day trip
Distance: 3 miles one way
Elevation gain: 1,400 feet; loss 200 feet
High point: 5,523 feet
Allow 1½ hours one way
Usually open late June through October
Topographic map:
  U.S.G.S. Battle Ax, Oreg.
  15'   1956

Although not an especially obvious landmark itself, the views from Bull of the Woods are outstanding, offering a panorama of peaks, greater and lesser, from Mt. Rainier to all of the Three Sisters. Another noteworthy feature of the hike is the summit lookout tower, a rarity since aerial surveillance has become the primary method of fire detection. Bull of the Woods is the hub of a network of trails, the shortest spoke being the one described here. So, hikers who want more of a workout or want to camp have many options such as trips to Big Slide Lake (see No. 48) and the Welcome Lakes or a side loop through Pansy Basin. The only source of water on the gentle climb is from small Terrance Spring at 1.9 miles.

Drive southeast of Estacada on Oregon 224 for 27 miles to a fork 0.5 mile beyond the Ripplebrook Ranger Station. Stay right on Road 46, following the sign to Bagby Hot Springs, and after 3.7 miles keep right on Road 63. After 5.7 miles along Road 63 keep right on Road 6340, as indicated by signs to Dickey Creek Trail, Bull of the Woods and Pansy Basin Trail. In 2.8 miles, where the pavement ends, stay right and then 5.3 miles farther turn left, following the sign to Bull of the Woods Trail. After 1.6 miles come to three forks, take the farthest right one and in 0.4 mile come to the signed trailhead on your right just before the road ends.

Switchback up through a slope of cleared blowdown, enter woods and walk at a levelish grade, passing a wee meadow and tarn. Switch back once at 0.6 mile and after a slight drop begin an easy uphill traverse. At 1.2 miles, a few yards beyond where the trail begins dropping, look left for a small metal tag on a tree pointing the way to North Dickey Peak. Hikers who enjoy easy cross country can climb for 0.2 mile to the open patch near the summit where the view includes the canyon holding Big Slide Lake and beyond to Olallie Butte, Mt. Jefferson and Three Fingered Jack. Try to follow approximately the same route back because the trees are considerably denser on either side of the tag, especially to the north.

The main trail continues traversing at a gentle, but irregular, grade. Pass above Terrace Spring and continue the series of up, down and level stretches to the junction of the connector to the trail into Pansy Lake Basin. This side loop past the lake and then up to Bull of the Woods would add about 3.5 miles and 1,200 feet of climbing.

For the remaining 0.9 mile to the summit Trail No. 550 continues traversing up the west side of the ridge at a moderate, but now persistent grade. A short distance beyond the junction pass through a small burn and then cross open slopes where you can peer down into Pansy Basin and then northwest to Table and Rooster Rocks (No. 46). Make two sets of switchbacks separated by a long traverse. As you walk along a treeless section of the ridge top have a preview of the landmarks you'll be able to study from the summit. Leave the crest and traverse along the west slope for the final distance to the junction just below the lookout. The trail that switchbacks down the south side of the peak soon meets a T-junction where a route goes west to Pansy Basin and Twin Lakes and another east to Big Slide and Welcome Lakes. Approximately 34,900 acres of the terrain extending below the summit became the Bull of the Woods Wilderness in 1984.

Bull of the Woods lookout

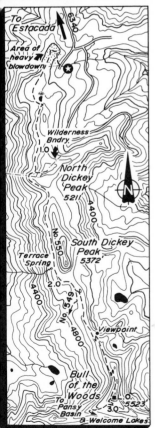

50 KUCKUP PARK

One day trip
**Distance: 1.4 miles one way; 0.7 mile
    additional to Viewpoint**
**Elevation gain: 350 feet; 250 feet additional
    to Viewpoint**
High point: 5,950 feet at Viewpoint
**Allow ¾ hour one way; ½ hour additional to
    Viewpoint**
Usually open July through mid October
Topographic map:
  U.S.G.S. Breitenbush Hot Springs, Oreg.
  15′   1961

Among trails in the Mt. Hood National Forest, one of the most exceptional routes is the short hike south from Breitenbush Lake to Kuckup Park. After traveling the length of a huge meadow and then climbing a bit in the woods the trail forks. One branch continues through woods to a viewpoint over rugged Shitiki Creek valley that is not visible to people taking the more popular Pacific Crest Trail that parallels the Kuckup Park Trail to the west. The other branch soon passes one of the best swimming lakes in the Cascades and continues on to several more.

If you're a fan of alpine swimming, the best time to make the hike is toward the end of August, just before the first cold snap. Although September will be too late for a comfortable swim, that is an excellent time for a visit, as it is for all high country. Of course, summer with its greens and wildflowers is also exquisite but then you'll encounter mosquitoes, the number and voraciousness of which are legendary in the Breitenbush Lake area. Unfortunately, no matter when you make the hike, you'll have the final 7.0 miles of driving along a road that is the worst approach to a trailhead in the Mt. Hood National Forest. It's not steep or particularly narrow but it is very rough and therefore slow going. People who feel they need more hiking than just the trip to Kuckup Park to justify that miserable drive can chose among several exceptionally scenic trips, such as following the PCT south toward Jefferson Park or heading north along the PCT and then looping back past Gibson Lake, a circuit of just under 4.0 miles.

From Estacada head southeast on Oregon 224 for 27 miles to a fork 0.5 mile beyond the Ripplebrook Ranger Station. Keep right on Road 46, follow it for 28 miles to Breitenbush Pass and turn left onto Road 4220. You also can reach Breitenbush Pass from Oregon 22 by taking Road 46 from Detroit for 17 miles. Allow 40 minutes to one hour to drive the 7.0 miles along unpaved 4220. After 6.9 miles pass signs marking where the PCT crosses the road. Continue another 0.1 mile to a parking area on your right just before the campground at Breitenbush Lake.

Walk to the southeast through the campground and along paths toward the stone shelter at the south end of Breitenbush Lake. About 125 feet before you actually reach the shelter come to a well defined, but unsigned, path that heads south along the edge of the huge meadow. Although not an official trail, you should have no trouble following it. The route of this hike, and for that matter Breitenbush Lake, are actually part of the Warm Springs Indian Reservation. Although the area continues to be managed the same as before the boundary change, keep in mind that you're a guest. Fisherman should note that they'll need a special fishing license to fish from any lakes in the reservation.

About 0.7 mile from the end of the lake pass a good source of water spouting from a pipe in the ground. Cross another small stream, leave the meadows and climb for a short distance through woods. A few hundred feet after you level off come to a fork where a big arrow has been cut into the trunk of a tree. To reach the viewpoint, stay right and climb at a reasonable grade through woods for 0.7 mile to overlooks above the valley holding Shitiki Creek. You may want to wander off the trail for a variety of perspectives.

To visit the lakes, turn left at the fork, after a few hundred yards of wee up, down and level stretches keep left at a branch and in a couple hundred feet come to that great swimming lake. Continue along the west and then a bit above the north sides to another lake from where you'll have a photogenic view of Mt. Jefferson. Continue even farther along the trail to large Lake Hilda. You can descend to Harvey Lake, although the terrain isn't quite as enticing.

Aerial view of Breitenbush Lake

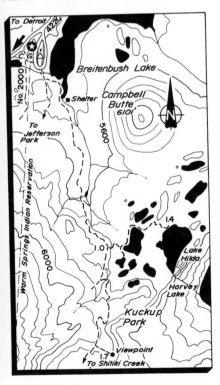

alphabetical index of trails

Cover Photos: Smugglers Cove
Pittock Mansion
Ponytail Falls